EXECUTING CRISIS

A C-Suite Crisis Leadership Survival Guide

Dr. Jo Robertson

ePub ISBN 978-1-944480-63-9
PDF eBook ISBN 978-1-944480-64-6
Print ISBN 978-1-944480-62-2

ROTHSTEIN PUBLISHING

A Division of Rothstein Associates Inc.

www.rothsteinpublishing.com

Dedication

To my husband, Steve,
who encouraged me to write this book.

ePub ISBN 978-1-944480-63-9
PDF eBook ISBN 978-1-944480-64-6
Print ISBN 978-1-944480-62-2

Library of Congress Control Number: 2019954962

A Division of Rothstein Associates Inc.

4 Arapaho Road
Brookfield, Connecticut 06804 USA
203.740.7400
info@rothstein.com
www.rothsteinpublishing.com

Preface

Over the course of my career as a management consultant, I have told my clients that they were really paying for all of the mistakes already made at someone else's expense. Lots of management gurus, entrepreneurs, sports pros, singers, actors and others have expounded on the value of learning from failure.

Of course, I would prefer learning from someone else's mistakes rather than my own – definitely more cost-effective, and as a management consultant admittedly sometimes more profitable.

But when those failures or mistakes are unavoidable, that's when it's *especially* critical to learn from others. Hands-on experience, training, exercising, talent, teamwork, resources and audit are all valuable, but when a black swan hisses in your face, learning from others is your best defense. And that's where Dr. Jo Robertson comes in.

Many books have been written on crisis management, crisis communication and, most critical when it hits the fan, *crisis leadership* – without doubt the most important factor in getting through any organizational crisis. I have dealt with more organizational crises over 35+ years of every manner, shape and size than I would care to recall, and yet, speaking with Jo and reading her writings, I have been surprised to realize that there is so much more I still have to learn.

This book is rich with real-world, first-hand case studies. Jo makes clear what worked in each crisis and, as important, what didn't work or at the least could have been better handled. She also shows how effective crisis leadership can make all the difference.

I challenge you to read this book and come away with the feeling that you already knew all the lessons Jo imparts herein. I dare you to believe you already know how to be the most effective crisis leader you could be. I encourage you to consider the consequences should you be wrong.

Read this book. Learn from someone who's been in your shoes and made the right choices when it hits the fan. Find out what you could do better when confronted with the crisis that can – and most likely will – make or break you and your organization sooner or later.

Philip Jan Rothstein, FBCI
October 2019

Foreword

If the world seems like it has become a more unpredictable and less forgiving place for corporations, it has. This is the new reality. Companies are increasingly in the headlines facing crises that may result from a single devastating event or a combination of escalating events or issues – major product failures, cyber breaches, reputational incidents, mass casualty events to name just a few.

The incidents and threats this book aims to provide solutions to, are not instances where the chess game is not going your way. Instead, someone has knocked over the pieces on the board, introduced new pieces from entirely different games, and in extreme situations changed or destroyed the board itself. Previous best practices are ineffective. The old rules do not apply. You cannot gather your best people and simply think your way through it. It's a new game. What you need are tools and a framework to get yourself and your organization though it and to above all protect the core assets of your business.

I met Dr. Jo Robertson almost twenty years ago at a small crisis management firm with a blue-chip client set. At the time, I was only beginning my career in crisis and emergency management. Jo was embarking on a second career on the other side of the camera. Previously she was a journalist utilizing tricks of the trade to capture that perfect sound bite from an executive whose world had just turned upside down (or was about to). She was now the firm's crisis communications leader, devising ways to help executives not only communicate effectively, but to make the right decisions so they had something worthy to communicate.

In the years that followed, we worked together analyzing corporate crises and supporting responses to real-time incidents. The majority of our work involved creating and conducting crisis simulations across major corporations. We built elaborate scenarios, laid traps, and executives fell in. Our exercises surfaced all the mistakes executives make and drove the lessons learned. We also observed proven tactics and learned new tactics from some of the savviest and most effective communicators and crisis managers across the Fortune 500.

I was amazed at how Jo was always calm, cool, and focused. The first thing you immediately recognize about Jo is her laser-like focus. The second is just how well she could think like corporate adversaries, be it the media or a relentless activist group. And how she knows how to neutralize them.

This book is not about theory or abstractions. It shares proven practices from an expert that has served as an adversary, as a crisis consultant to the largest corporations in the world, and as an in-house crisis manager across numerous industries. Jo shares her firsthand experiences dealing with numerous incidents and what it was like in the moment, preparing, and acting to control the situation.

The book begins by making the crucial distinction between day to day communication and crisis communication. It then digs into key tactics and practices for effective crisis communications, including key actions before an incident occurs that can put you in a better position when a crisis strikes. This is proactive crisis communications at its core.

In the same vein, the book then provides practical tips for preparing an organization to manage a crisis including building teams and the ever important, but often overlooked, concept of operations. It also debunks some of the cardinal rules of business continuity that organizations have followed because…well… it's always been that way. It then turns to questions around the use of apologies, an area often misstated in the academic research and by some of the big PR firms. Finally, the last two chapters look at best practice on media training and executing the communications strategy. This includes key pitfalls to avoid and advanced methods to shape the narrative and utilize what some may see as unwanted coverage to your advantage.

My entire career has focused on helping organizations proactively engage risks and manage uncertainty when the world turns upside down and then inside out. I've worked with more than seventy companies across a variety of industries to develop crisis preparedness. What I've learned is that crises happen to good companies. And great management teams fail because they are good at day to day management, not at crisis management. But the good news is that through pre-planning, training, and practicing (exercises) executive teams can become effective at crisis management.

The crises Jo Robertson addresses in this book aren't temporary obstacles organizations face. The stakes are far higher. These crises pose a threat to the very viability of the organization itself, and typically impose permanent change onto the organization, oftentimes regardless of how we respond. The key variable is how much influence we are able to employ over the crisis and if we are able to affect a positive change or if we succumb to a negative one.

It's not about putting the chessboard back together. It's about employing tactics to adapt the organization to a new game no matter what the rules are. The tips and tools shared in this book are critical for executives to effectively manage and communicate during these situations, a critical step to survive and even thrive in crisis situations.

Larry Cristini

Head of Global Crisis Management

Facebook

September 2019

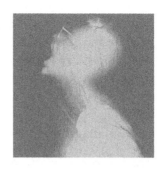

Table of Contents

Introduction

After years of working with companies in a wide variety of industries to help them manage crises, I have realized that many otherwise thoroughly savvy executives don't take the potential for crisis as seriously as they should. They may have great disaster recovery plans, or they might be following so-called best practices in crisis management, but they are still woefully underprepared.

There are a lot of good reasons for this. A lot of the time, folks at the top of companies have gotten there because their business instincts are really good, and when it comes to crises, a whole lot of people, especially entrepreneurs, have dealt with short-term emergencies and critical incidents throughout their careers. Seat-of-the-pants reactions to tough situations have gotten them through difficulties before and they assume that will continue to be the case.

But white-knuckling through a lean period when you're not sure that you can make payroll is a whole different situation than an emergency that the company may have had a hand in creating.

In the more than two decades that I've been doing this work, I've met plenty of C-suite consultants who have virtually no crisis training. **Business leaders would be better served by understanding key crisis concepts and applying them to their own situation rather than relying on crisis advisors to swoop in to take care of a problem once it has become a crisis.**

That is what this book sets out to do. It is intended as a manual to assist you – the savvy leader – to make your organization more resilient to crisis.

An organization, large or small, may face many different risks that could disrupt its operations or ability to do business, including natural disasters such as hurricanes, tornadoes, and earthquakes, emergency events like fire, terrorism, facility accidents, civil unrest, pandemics, disruptions to the supply chain… management malfeasance… the list goes on. It is not necessary in most cases to ensure a definitive list has been analyzed in order to prepare for the potentialities. Ongoing business continuity planning for getting back in operation following a disruption is an essential element of risk management, as is being prepared to respond to an emergency situation that can affect life, health, or safety at one of your organization's facilities. But whether the crisis management program includes one interwoven plan with tactical and strategic components throughout the lifecycle of the event or multiple plans synched to work in harmony, is immaterial.

What's the difference between risk management and crisis management? What's the difference between crisis management and business continuity? How do you ensure you've got the important strategic elements covered?

Sometimes the whole caboodle is called *business continuity management*. The term has become very popular and has been driven by the business continuity and disaster recovery industry, which came of age in the 1990s. Another term is *resilience*. Unfortunately, (as of this writing) that term tends to refer primarily to business resumption—or the process of planning for how the organization will get back to normal operations as quickly as possible following a disruption. It seems to be less about making the organization resilient against crises to begin with.

I prefer the umbrella term *crisis management*. Whatever you call it – emergency response, business continuity, disaster recovery – crisis communication, and crisis management plans, elements, tactics and strategies all need to work together seamlessly for an organization to truly be resilient.

This book is meant to be simple and easy to grasp immediately. The concepts are relevant for most organizations. Still, there is no one-size-fits-all when it comes to crisis plans, strategy, or response. There are numerous good crisis manuals available and I don't seek to repeat the material you will find elsewhere. Instead, I will supplement with new twists on "best practice" – to update the common understanding of what elevates good crisis management beyond wordsmithing.

Instead of lists of the items that are "necessary" for a solid crisis plan or well-stocked war room, you'll find key things to consider as you tailor strategies for your own organization. In fact, I'm going to shoot down best practices that are outdated yet continue to be repeated because someone somewhere decided they were best practices. Who gets to determine what is best practice in the first place? It's time for a little fresh thinking and common sense. It's really critical to do the right thing up front, which, in a lot of cases can prevent crises. Instead, a lot of people continue to conflate crisis communication with obfuscation and pretty words intended to make a very bad situation seem less bad without actually doing anything to make it better. That's public relations. It is not good crisis communication. And crisis communication is not crisis management. Certainly, communication is a strong component, and having people who have been media-trained and can represent a company well in a crisis is important. But there's so much more to managing a crisis well. **No successful crisis response begins when the crisis begins.**

And finally, a thought on best practices: they are most effective for things that people do all the time. Posting a hand-sanitizer dispenser on the wall near the door of a patient's hospital room that people can use when they come and go is a great practice. And it's one that you can amend as you go because people do it all the time. But crisis management is something you don't do many times a day.

Best practices for activities that we do all day, every day, can naturally evolve more easily because of the frequency with which people do them. It's the very infrequency (let's hope) of crises that makes them harder to establish and maintain best practices for. A crisis management best practice from three years ago may not be the right choice for managing a crisis today, and it might not be the right solution for your situation. It is time to challenge best practices.

To give a personal example, many years ago my father had to have surgery. Like all fairly serious medical situations, it had the possibility of turning out really badly. So that he didn't worry his adult children, siblings, or mother, my dad decided he would keep us in the dark until the day of the surgery. Even though we were all well-educated, competent professional adults, my parents' generation's "best practice" was to keep people in the dark until after it was over to save them from unnecessary worry.

Fortunately, it all went well. However, it got me to thinking about how awful it was to be kept in the dark. Family is hugely important to me and I remember dropping everything and driving 4+ hours to be there at the hospital so that, yes, I could just stand around and worry. I was glad to have been able to make the decision myself to be present in the waiting room during the surgery – it was a choice my grandmother did not get to make. My parents, however well-meaning, took that possibility away from her.

But they were going by the book. So, in a sense, I am writing this book to let you know that sometimes it's just the wrong thing to do to go by the book.

I started out not to write a manual for crisis management, but to challenge what dabblers believed were best practices, to update and create better guidance for executives, and to provide plenty of common-sense examples of better practice in play. By doing so, I hope I have provided you with the guidance and tools you'll need to weather any crisis!

Dr. Jo Robertson

October 2019

CHAPTER 1

DAY-TO-DAY BUSINESS COMMUNICATION VS. CRISIS COMMUNICATION

You're a small business owner – you own a little coffee shop in a swanky part of town near a well-known and highly respected university. You have sunk everything you have into this business. You've found the best roaster you can, you have yummy snacks and sandwiches. You bought the business from the previous owner, but you've staked everything and expanded, and are looking to expand further. Business is good. You've got a lot of loyal customers. Your shop has been broken into twice – and it turned out to be a former employee who you fired because he had a drug problem and you caught him stealing. Most often the biggest issue you have had to deal with is a sick employee.

The shop has a great atmosphere, funky university chic. You have five employees, two of whom are full-time, and you pay them well enough to keep them because they're good people and you can count on both of them to step up when you need them. The others are part-timers, although you have a bit of an issue keeping the part-timers because of the shift work. Still, it's very close to a family atmosphere. You know all of them well. Some of them, you know their families.

Generally, you open the shop at five each morning, so you're usually there at 4:30 because you want to have coffee ready when you open the doors to your regulars.

One morning in the spring, you arrive to open up, and things seem a little odd. One of your full-timers, Jim, was scheduled to close up last night, but things don't seem to have been locked up the way they normally would be. Maybe you're a little angry at Jim when you unlock the door and head toward the back. But then suddenly you know why the lights are still on because right there, next to the cash register, is Jim's body. You've been trained in CPR, so you check to see if he has a pulse. He does not. Quickly, you check the rest of your shop. Two of your part-timers are also dead. You call 911 and report the crime.

You go outside and sit on the curb, in shock, and wait for the police. You've watched enough TV to know that you shouldn't mess with the crime scene any more than you already have.

It's not your first crisis, but it is likely the biggest you will ever face. Now, cold-blooded as it may seem, you need to communicate. What do you do?

This is not a true story; however, a similar situation did happen, and it's an example I use in the classes I teach about crisis communications. It happened in a Starbucks in the Georgetown area of Washington, DC. But it also could happen anywhere, and as a corporation, Starbucks has different resources than a small businessperson would. It also happened a decade before the iPhone was introduced, and more than a decade before social media.

You have a crisis on your hands, you need to communicate, and you need to communicate sooner than later. What do you do?

This chapter covers:

- *Planning a communications campaign in a day-to-day environment vs. crisis communications.*
- *Crafting "hip pocket" statements today for the crisis tomorrow.*
- *Why and how to communicate at the speed of sound.*
- *Reframing the issue to move forward.*

1.1 Everyday Communication vs. Communicating During Crisis

Crisis communications and conventional business communications are different, so it first makes sense to look at how conventional business communications work.

In a day-to-day business environment, communications and public relations team members have the luxury of time to plan out their environment. They'll strategize how best to market their products and services and how to highlight their wares to best effect. Typically, a marketing plan for a new product launch will include the following standard elements:[1]

- *Situation* – what is the situation that led to the conclusion that a PR program was needed?
- *Objective* – what is the outcome the organization wants to achieve?
- *Audience* – who is the organization trying to reach? (The more specific, the better. "General public" makes a lousy target audience because identifying what will appeal to such a broad group may render tactics that are scattershot.)
- *Strategy* – how is the objective going to be achieved? What are the guidelines for the program?
- *Tactics* – what are the specific activities and sequence to put the plan into operation? (What messages need to be communicated? What vehicles will best get that message to that audience?)
- *Budget*

- *Timetable (or calendar)* – plan out how long it will take for each step… as well as when to initiate the campaign
- *Measurement criteria* – this ties back to the objective. How does the organization determine whether its communication plan was effective (and, if it fell short, what tweaks to the strategy are needed?)

Let's say, for example, that you've decided you want to open a coffee shop in Georgetown, an upscale neighborhood in Washington DC where Georgetown University is located. Perhaps we might sketch out our communications campaign elements something like this:

Situation – You want to open a coffee shop one block off campus that will appeal to Georgetown students.

Objective – to drive Georgetown University students to frequent your coffee shop instead of nearby (and plentiful) competitors. You also intend to have a very aggressive sales objective of matching your competitors' profits within the first month.

Audience – current students. (Although you certainly won't turn away nearby residents and business customers, students are the primary audience to which you wish to appeal).

Strategy – You want to become *the* place where Georgetown University students go to hang out. You want them to swing by first thing in the morning… and to come back between classes. You want them to come in to study or to work on team projects or to relax in the evenings. You want them to bring their friends.

Tactics – What's going to appeal to this demographic and how do you reach them to share the news about this new outpost? Your seating needs to be comfortable; you need to offer free Wi-Fi and plenty of outlets to recharge phones and laptops, coffee should be good (and fair trade) and not too expensive. You might think about snacks and sandwiches. Perhaps offer live music on Friday evenings. Maybe student art for sale on the walls… And to reach out to them using social media to keep them abreast of upcoming events, product launches and specials. You'll reward them for liking your shop or introducing someone from their network.

Social media can also be a great way to gather metrics. For example, how many customers signed up for and used the coupon. What are people on Yelp! saying?

Budget – Add up the cost of the tactics you're pitching. Don't forget to include the cost of the employee time to keep your social media channels fresh.

Timetable – How long will it take to implement this effectively? Will you have everything ready to go on the first day of Fall semester?

Measurement criteria – What were your profits the first month following launch? Did you match the profits of your local competitors? If not, what do you need to tweak to make this communication plan more effective?

But all of this has taken place in a day-to-day environment, where the communications professionals on your team have had the luxury of time to think through and plan out your communications campaign.

It's a vastly different situation when there's been a crisis!

1.2 Communicating in Crisis

In the summer of 1997, three employees at a Starbucks coffee shop in Georgetown were murdered overnight.[2] It came as a shock to the DC neighborhood, to customers, and employees. I'm sure it was a shock to the Starbucks leadership team as well.

In this case, the coffee shop was well established, not a start-up. And it belonged to the well-known Starbucks chain. But the impact is similar even if the scale is completely different. If this had been your new, startup coffee shop, would it have mattered to your customers that you had comfortable furniture, Wi-Fi, fair trade coffee at reasonable prices? Would your billing of your establishment as the go-to place for Georgetown University students be enough to keep your clientele coming back in the weeks following the incident, or would there be other factors affecting their decision to frequent (or not) your business?

It would stand to reason that security might rise to the top of the list of customer concerns. This was a neighborhood where clientele had never given security a second thought, and at least until the suspects were in custody and motive was sorted out, customers could hardly be blamed for turning elsewhere, right? Why not go back to the competitor down the street, rather than chance it or get involved in making a stand?

So certainly, security is an issue that has to be dealt with head on. But it is not the issue you – as a business leader – want your customers to continue to focus on as the weeks drag on (and especially not after the situation has been resolved). More on that in just a little bit.

The most pressing difference between communicating in a crisis situation is a lack of time to prepare what to say *before* leadership must begin communicating about the crisis. So let's talk about that first.

This particular situation happened a decade before the introduction of the iPhone, and the social networking that ensued. Had it happened today, arriving customers would certainly have whipped out their phones to not only take pictures but to broadcast the images and their own take on the "news" as far as their social media channels would take the information. That would have even keener impacts on the coffee shop's ability to frame the issue or to connect directly with impacted customers.

A generation ago, it was considered best practice for a company in crisis to respond before the next news cycle. Typically (in the United States, at least) that meant the major 6pm or 11pm news broadcasts.

To put that in plainer terms, companies often had the better part of a day to figure out what to say and to polish it up. Twenty years ago, when this event occurred, CNN's continuous broadcasts had shrunk that news cycle considerably and the rule of thumb for a company in crisis was to begin communicating within one hour. Today, primarily as a result of social media, a company in crisis needs to be prepared to begin communicating immediately or risk loss of control of the message as untrained citizen journalists step in to fill the space with what they believe they have witnessed and often with no real attempt at verification of facts.

As a side note, I often teach classes for business executives who have come to the United States for an intensive week-long course on how business works in this country. After discussion of the Georgetown coffee crisis, I usually ask students how long, if they had been the owners of the business, they think they would have to begin communicating.

"Within 24 hours" invariably is the first answer. Business leaders take note: You do not have 24 hours. You do not have one hour. (That's usually the second answer.) You must begin communicating immediately.

This is extremely hard to do. Think about it. First of all, there's the shock and horror of employees being murdered in your shop. There's a police investigation to deal with, which means the business will be closed until the police are finished. It also means that the establishment will be surrounded with yellow tape, which would be a very good advertisement for folks with cameras to start taking pictures. Which also means that from here on into perpetuity, there will be images online of your shop surrounded by yellow police tape.

So, in your shock and horror, what information are you likely to be able to get immediately after the start of the crisis? The police may work with you to gather evidence, but they are much less likely to share with you what information they have gathered in any sort of immediate way.

One thing that you can be sure of is that the information you can get will be incomplete. There will be a great deal of uncertainty. You don't want to circulate rumors but waiting for all the facts to be in before doing anything leaves a void that invariably will be filled with misinformation.

A small television crew arrives, or a reporter with a camera. You have to say something, so what do you say?

1.3 Have a Statement in Your Hip Pocket

Here are a few statements you can craft now and have in your hip pocket and which, with cursory on-the-spot tailoring, will work for this kind of situation:

- **Statement of whatever facts we know right now**. ("Our hearts are broken. We arrived this morning to find that three of our employees and friends had been murdered. We are a small

11

business, and this is like losing family. We are working with the
police to help in their investigation, and when we have more
information, we will share it with you. Our hearts and prayers go
out to the families of our friends and coworkers.)

- **What you are doing to get more information.** ("We are
  working collaboratively with law enforcement to provide them
  with access to anything which will help in their ability to
  determine what happened, who did this, and why.")

- **Empathy**. The importance of this element cannot be overstated…
  and should be stated within the first 30 seconds of opening your
  mouth or you will lose your audience. You must acknowledge the
  human aspects of how this affects you personally. It's
  humanizing. Without formally realizing it, the audiences you are
  speaking to are holding their breath (and not listening fully) until
  you show your human side. ("This is a sad day for us, and we are
  in shock. Please allow us a little space to grieve along with the
  families of our colleagues who were lost.")

- **When you will be back to provide more information.** ("I am
  going inside now to meet with officers and get more details. I will
  brief you again – right here – at 11am.")

The true value of stepping forward to communicate when you don't
really have much more than this to communicate, is that it puts a stake in
the sand and establishes your organization as being forthcoming with
accurate information. Although it is unlikely to stop the rumors
completely, it will help minimize them.

1.4 Case Studies on Communicating Quickly

Quick communication is important… but so is accuracy and accessibility.
Ensure you hit the target on all counts.

1.4.1 DuPont La Porte (November 15, 2014)

Initial communication from DuPont following an early morning methyl
mercaptan (MeSH) leak in La Porte, Texas that killed four employees
was not quick and may have taken as long as twelve hours. It is difficult

to determine what was initially posted since all links appear to now lead to the updated and polished statement provided two days later.

Early media reports indicate Plant Manager Randall Clements issued an interim written holding statement that failed to reassure. The statement said the company was cooperating with federal, state and local authorities, and was conducting its own inquiry. "We will share what we learn with relevant authorities," Clements said. The New York Times (and other media) reported that Clements could not be reached for further comment in the hours that followed.[3]

Although DuPont's LaPorte plant uses MeSH to manufacture pesticides, DuPont's carefully crafted official statement[4] appeared to downplay the hazard, misleadingly indicating their MeSH is instead used as a natural gas odorant. (See paragraph 3 in the DuPont statement.)

Figure 1-1 DuPont Statement on La Porte (Texas) Facility Incident (11/17/14)

The media didn't focus a lot of time on the specific dangers of methyl mercaptan because DuPont's misleading characterization of the chemical left them with the assumption that it was no more dangerous than the odorant used in natural gas.

It may be interesting to note that DuPont's LaPorte plant also manufactures methyl isocyanate – the chemical tied to the Bhopal tragedy in India in 1984 which killed thousands. Public outrage following Bhopal (and more recently the West Fertilizer explosion in West, Texas on April 17, 2013) have led the government to seek greater chemical plant safety and security protocols.[5]

Lesson learned: don't downplay danger at the expense of accurate information. Downplaying danger can lead to public outrage and a feeling of being "played" when the truth comes out.

Speedy statements are just as important as getting it right. As this next case study shows, if the company doesn't start communicating immediately, someone else will….

1.4.2 Exxon Torrance Explosion and Fire (February 15, 2015)

Nearby residents and community members were told to shelter-in-place following an explosion at the Exxon refinery in Torrance, California in February 2015. Within a couple of hours, the company acknowledged the incident and explained they were focusing on accounting for personnel and evaluating the cause, though initial media reports noted that the company was not immediately available for comment.

"*The company was not immediately available for comment*" is an open invitation for eyewitnesses (with no formal chemistry training) to use social media channels to frame events and spread news, photos, and opinions – leaving the company to play catch up. Here is some of what was said on social media before Exxon began communicating:

Possible damage caused by the explosion at the Torrance Exxon Refinery. #Torrance
pic.twitter.com/cdkq5SoKmN via: @jenniferthang

🐦 LANCE ULANOFF @LANCEULANOFF · 3 MONTHS AGO

Figure 1-2. Possible damage caused by the explosion of the Torrance Exxon Refinery. # Torrance. pic.twitter.com/cdkq55oKmN via @jenniferthang Lance Ulanoff @lanceulanoff

---

Ricardo Segura
@rik944
Hope everyone is ok at or near the refinery explosion
@exxonmobil in Torrance, CA #dangerousairquality

Local Guy
I have samples of this "ash" people think. It is NOT ash. It's NOT fire suppression material either. Looks like fibers… and truthfully, looks like Asbestos to me. Unless Exxon Mobile steps it up and tells us what the heck was showered all over South Bay, I would recommend we all be careful with it. I'd love to have someone get it checked out to find out the truth too. Exxon Mobile says they don't know what it is… yet. Meanwhile it looks like the white stuff covered their building and the smashed minivan in the destruction photo… so they sure had a

---

15

Akemi Tachibana
@UnAmericanOtaku

It really looks like a volcano blew up right in the middle of #Torrance. Ash and destruction EVERYWHERE.

Rusty Goodcat

I hope the white stuff floating all over is not Asbestos!

SharkAttack23

This is the result of scabs working the refinery.

The real refinery workers were on strike, and Exxon brought in scabs to replace the striking workers.

Lesson learned: if the company doesn't step forward with an explanation and accurate information quickly, there are plenty of people who will opine with conviction over what happened and why, whether they know what happened or not.

1.5 Reframing the Issue

Getting back to the issue of the coffee shop customers' concerns about security following a shooting, it's clear the speed of communication is among the most important elements of crisis response. But as the crisis works its way through the most immediate phase and becomes an ongoing story, leadership will want to turn its attention more toward refocusing the concerns of stakeholders on something they can control and how they can play a part in the solution. It can be a very important element in reframing the crisis from what went wrong (or what the organization failed at) to a path forward toward healing.

In the case of the Starbucks shooting in 1997, the company did a marvelous job of reframing the issue to refocus away from a perception that their shop was less secure or more dangerous – or even that it had a bad lingering vibe because of the deaths – and built goodwill while they rebuilt their customer base.

CEO Howard Shultz cut short his vacation and flew to Washington DC to be with employees. Starbucks invited the families of the slain victims to sit down with them to brainstorm how they could memorialize the three employees who had died, and they implemented the best ideas, including:

- Making the store a living memorial to the three slain employees with a floor-to-ceiling mural with the employees' initials and photos.
- Offering a $100,000 reward for the apprehension of the murderers.
- Paying for the funerals of the victims.

But the final idea took the cake: announcing that all net profits would go to a foundation that promotes nonviolence.

The net result was a shift in perception. No longer did customers avoid the shop because of what happened. Instead they returned feeling like they were able to take an active part in showing support for the victims of violence in a meaningful way by patronizing the establishment instead of staying away.

Summary

Planning a communications campaign in a day-to-day environment is vastly different from planning to communicate during a crisis. You will not have the luxury of time, and must begin communicating immediately, even if you do not have all the facts. Crafting your "hip pocket" statements today for tomorrow's crisis can help.

Questions for Further Thought and Discussion

- *The last time you were spokesperson for your organization, how long did it take between when the crisis occurred and when you made a statement to the press?*
- *What are the "hip pocket" statements (see section 1.3) you can craft right now to pull out in the event there is another crisis at your organization?*
- *Realistically, how quickly do you believe you will be able to begin communicating if you use these hip pocket statements as a guide?*
- *What other steps can you take to narrow the distance between when an incident happens and when you are able to begin communicating about it?*

CHAPTER 2

OVERVIEW OF CRISIS COMMUNICATION

Unfolding crises may often be characterized by confusion. Information may be conflicting and there is a lot of interest in what is happening. Without adequate communication, the story can easily become mired in misinformation. Rumors abound.[6]

On the other hand, effective communication despite the challenges can elevate your organization's response above excuse-making to provide vital information to stakeholders (rather than forcing them to choose whether to believe rumors) and demonstrates that your organization's leadership is in charge. It will aid your ability to remain in business, and it points the press in a more positive direction (rather than chasing rabbit holes trying to figure out what is really happening).

Let's take a look at how to begin structuring your organization's crisis communication capability.

This chapter covers:

- *Working with the media, including traditional media as well as social media dynamics.*
- *A discussion of the most critical elements that make communication with the media effective.*
- *Tactics for mitigating crises where your organization may be to blame.*

2.1 Working With the Media

Why wouldn't you? The number one reason that comes to mind (every time I do media training, this issue comes up) is "No matter what I say, they'll quote me out of context" [See section 9.1.4 in the chapter on Media Training for a technique to take control of that].

The media are a primary means to get critical information to many of your key audiences quickly (though it can be a less than perfect way to communicate with employees). They may know your stakeholders better than you do because they have not only researched their demographics but have keen experience putting themselves in their audiences' shoes to determine what interests them most. Plus, most legitimate media pride themselves on objectivity and aren't consumed with pushing a particular viewpoint the way an organization in trouble often seeks to paint its side of the story in pretty colors. (Note please that I am talking about old-fashioned news journalists from credible news organizations and not commentators or talk show hosts.)

Finally, the media is going to be there whether we want them to or not.[7]

We've already discussed the need for speed in beginning your communication. But *who* are you communicating with and how do you best approach them? What are the nuances that don't play in your favor, especially in a crisis environment?

2.1.1 Television

- Broadcast updates as the situation evolves.
- Editing is critical – corrections are not likely to be seen by the same audience[8].

This means it's a never-ending shell game. A television reporter may begin a breaking news story with "Details are sketchy, but…" This is typically followed by rumors gleaned from "eyewitnesses" on site who may or may not have any real knowledge. Reporters typically justify this because they've reached out to the organization for comment and have not yet heard back. Reporters have deadlines. Something big has happened and they have to have it on their air or on their pages. Remember, you may have only minutes before the first broadcast hits. In most cases your organization's communications personnel will still be scrambling to wordsmith an official statement unless you've planned in advance what you can say when you know little or nothing. (See the previous chapter to eliminate this from happening at your organization.)

Alternately, the official spokesperson is not immediately available for comment and company employees on scene are not authorized to comment. (Would it be worth considering authorizing any employee to comment during crisis as long as they stick with the facts, don't repeat rumor, and talk from the pre-scripted templates we developed in the last chapter? [More on this in section 10.8.]

However, television news audiences can be mercurial. They may catch a few minutes while cooking the kids' breakfast in the morning or while passing by a screen tuned to a news channel during the day. Because of that, 24/7 television news shows often cycle through the big news stories of the day, with updates as they come in. So, an audience that heard rumors or misinformation when the story first broke may not be in attendance when additional facts and corrections get added at the next update. In fact, the audience that originally heard the misinformation, may *never* learn their understanding of the "facts" is faulty. As leaders in our organizations, we can't afford to take the chance that some portion of the audience got inaccurate news because we weren't prepared to start communicating right away.

2.1.2 Radio

- Generally one person.
- Must tell the story with audio only[9].

This means radio reporters have fewer resources than other broadcast brethren. Although many TV reporters – especially in smaller markets – shoot, edit and report themselves, radio reporters have always been a one-man band. They don't typically have a crew to help them capture the story or facilitate news gathering. And they've got to paint a picture with their eyes closed – twice as hard.

2.1.3 Daily newspapers

- More in-depth.
- Provide background that broadcast stories don't[10].

Newspapers *used* to be more in depth. But that was in the days before major newspapers had dot-com versions of themselves, so it's not necessarily a truism anymore. In the past, newspapers had the luxury of continuing to gather news throughout the evening before finally publishing and distributing overnight. Today, online editors are forced to keep pace with their broadcast counterparts to publish first and continually update.

2.1.4 Weekly magazines

- Go beyond the basics – adding detail and analysis.
- More time to verify and obtain information[11].

2.1.5 Internet

- Often the first place people go for information on an unfolding incident.
- Under competitive pressure to post first and check facts later; fact-checking is often nonexistent.
- Copy editing not stringent, sometimes nonexistent.
- Can spread misinformation quickly and globally in minutes.
- Similar to 24/7 broadcast news channels.
- Makes international coverage as accessible as local coverage.
- Interactivity – webcasts, chat rooms, blogs, links to other organizations for more information and resources[12].

There remain some minor nuances between the types of media traditional journalists use to tell their stories, but the internet increasingly minimizes the differences. Perhaps the biggest dynamic of all is what social media is doing to traditional media.

2.2 Social Media Dynamics

Social media and new media dynamics are constantly changing, but as of 2017:

- 7% of the US population used social media 10 years ago.
- 65%+ of the US population uses social media today.
- Including 90% of young adults.
- Seniors are the quickest growing sector.
- The average US person spends two hours on social media every day[13].

Recent statistics indicate:

- One in every seven people on earth is on Facebook[14].
- 400+ hours of videos are posted on YouTube every minute[15].
- Social media accounts for more than 1/3 of all time spent online in the US[16].

2.2.1 Socialnomics

Self-appointed "Socialnomics" guru Erik Qualman claims in a fascinating video clip on the impact of social media that New Yorkers received tweets about the east coast earthquake of 2011 (which originated in Virginia), thirty seconds before they felt it… and that Lady Gaga, Justin Bieber, and Katy Perry have more Twitter followers than the entire populations of Germany, Turkey, South Africa, Canada, Argentina, and Egypt.

Qualman has redone the video to keep up with the stats, but I think the 2013 version is still the most powerful:

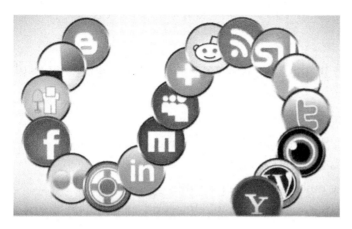

Fig. 2-1. Erik Qualman's Socialnomics video clip can be found at
https://www.youtube.com/watch?v=N4znQDyz038

2.2.2 Traditional Media Embrace

Twitter started as a free service that allowed people to keep in touch
through the exchange of quick, frequent updates on what they were doing
through text-based posts to the Twitter website or via SMS for anyone
who had signed up for the information. It was meant to be a means for
friends and family to keep in contact.

That all changed in April 2009 when screen star Ashton Kutcher
challenged CNN to see which would be the first Twitter account to
achieve one million followers. Kutcher won the @aplush vs. @CNN
battle. It was the first time the traditional media sat up and took notice of
social media. Until that point, traditional media believed it had all the
tools it needed to reach its audiences on its own terms.

The Iranian elections two months later (June 2009) solidified the use of
social media as a tool used by the traditional media.

The election between incumbent Ahmadinejad and rival Mousavi was
turbulent and the win for Ahmadinejad led to violent riots across Iran,
charges of voting fraud, and protests worldwide. The Iranian government
jammed cell phones and text messages, and blocked access to social
networking sites to keep the information from being reported.

Twitter was harder to block because of its decentralized framework. It
enabled an online community within Iran to convey information to

protesters (as well as the rest of the world) who were shut off from independent news sources. Citizentube (a YouTube channel) allowed users to upload their own news coverage.

Traditional media caved and since then is more likely to take a position of "if you can't beat them join them." You will see news stations actively eliciting eyewitness reports and audience engagement and participation in the reporting of news.

A number of years ago, the Dallas Fox affiliate acknowledged and poked fun at its embrace of social media, with this tongue-in-cheek encouragement to link with them:

Fig. 2-2 Video clip of Dallas Fox affiliate poking fun at its embrace of social media can be found at http://www.youtube.com/watch?v=O8g3AFnT_Hk

The point is this: Social media can't be ignored. It facilitates global communication – for traditional media, as well as untrained citizen journalists who abide by no particular code of conduct, have no journalistic training or degree, with no editor breathing down their neck to report "both" sides, and no requirement to substantiate the information they allege. In the past, traditional media generally took honor in – at a minimum – vetting their sources and attempting to objectively report a balanced truth.

Business and organizational leaders must now take into consideration communication with and through social media as part of their platform. Although we discuss communication with the "media" throughout this book, "media" now must be inclusive of social media too, not just traditional journalists.

Despite this mandate, it is not likely you will have the resources to communicate through all social media channels. To attempt to do so can be scattershot and thin. Instead, analyze what channels your key audiences use and plan to prioritize the top two or three. If your communications team is large, add a few more, but don't add so many you can't adequately keep each platform fresh.

2.2.3. Analyzing Which Platforms to Use

Analyze not only what platforms are most popular in general, but what platforms are most popular with your demographic. For example, in the infographic below which summarizes the world's most popular platforms, non-Asian users may not be familiar with Asia's most popular platforms (QQ, QZONE).

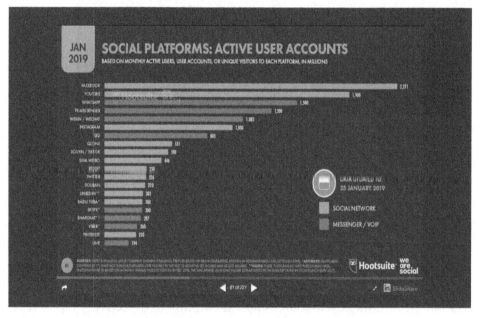

Fig. 2-3. Detail on the most popular social media channels can be found at
https://wearesocial.com/global-digital-report-2019

The infographic in Fig. 2-3[17] provides a snapshot more closely focused on the French population, to highlight some of the country-by-country differences. Though Snapchat may trend high among US teens, it wouldn't necessarily be the best channel for a French company to put its resources into, especially if the organization doesn't pitch its products to teenagers.

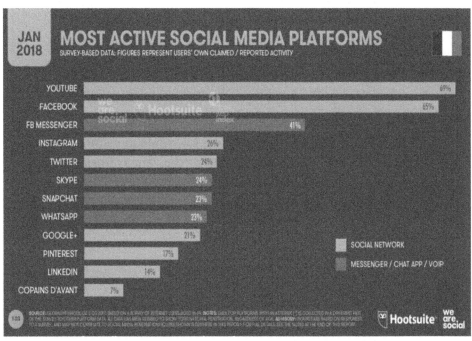

Fig. 2-4. Detail on the most popular platforms in France can be found at https://www.slideshare.net/wearesocial/digital-in-2018-in-northern-europe-part-1-west-86864045

Always look for the most recent social media data you can get your hands on because the dynamics are constantly in flux and social media platforms can go in and out of style as quickly as clothing fashions. Although MySpace was a big deal when the Dallas Fox affiliate put together the self-deprecating clip referenced earlier, its popularity waned quickly as newer platforms came into favor. Figure out the top social media platforms for your location and your demographic and focus your social media efforts on communicating with your audiences using those mediums.

2.2.4 Don't Delegate Social Media to Junior Staff

One more word of caution on communicating emergency information through social media. Don't leave this to the most junior staff member or newest millennial hire. Plenty of middle-aged execs like to wash their hands of having to learn the social media ropes and instead delegate the monitoring and communicating through these platforms. But this can backfire in a couple of ways.

First, junior staffers may not yet have accumulated the business acumen to make sound decisions or keep the conversation polite when provoked. And for this reason, they may not be empowered with the authority needed to post on behalf of the organization.

Fig. 2-5 provides an example of an ASUS fail when launching its new computer product at a major 2012 industry expo. The Bernstein Crisis Management blog captured the photo and comment ASUS used on Twitter, as well as the backlash from the frat boy-like communication[18]:

Fig. 2.5. ASUS "fail" courtesy of Bernstein Crisis Management blog at *https://managementhelp.org/blogs/crisis-management/2012/06/10/asus-fails-at-social-media/*

However, needing to have the text of all crisis postings vetted with more senior staff can significantly hamper the organization's ability to get communications out quickly. [More on this in section 4.2 on approvals.]

2.2.5 Quick and Transparent

This 17-minute TedX Talk by Melissa Agnes[19] discussing the secret to successful crisis management in the 21st Century could be useful. (Hint: In case you haven't guessed it by now, her answer is: *speedy and transparent communication utilizing social media*.) Melissa Agnes says building trust and credibility with the stakeholder groups that are most important by empowering team members to connect with these stakeholders through social channels, increases your ability to reach your key audiences directly because the tools are already in your (and your stakeholders') pockets.

Fig. 2-6 Melissa Agnes video clip can be found at https://www.youtube.com/watch?v=VQGEPEaEWtg

2.3 What Makes Communication with the Media Effective?

Speed and accuracy. Crisis response and communication must be immediate despite limited information. Minutes after an incident, the media (traditional and social) will be pushing for accurate information from the organization.

Honesty and sincerity. Practice open and honest communication. Does the spokesperson believe what they are saying? Stakeholders will critique every decision and statement and look for hidden meaning and intentions, and public perception of whether you (or your spokesperson) is being forthright will play a big role in whether your organization's communication is effective.

Journalists will judge whether they believe your spokesperson is telling the truth. Is s/he looking you in the eye or reading from a prepared script? [See Brown's Bar case study in section 8.9.] Is his or her body language tense and uncomfortable? Is she or he perspiring far beyond what would be warranted by the weather? Is she or he clearly unfamiliar, unprepared, or unpracticed as a spokesperson? Do they lack a sense of empathy and seem oblivious to the plight of those caught in the wake of their event? Do they appear to be defending rather than explaining? The public generally responds more favorably to organizations that show a human side and sincerely acknowledge messing up.

2.3.1 Case Study: Freedom Industries' Elk River Chemical Spill (January 9, 2014)

This Freedom Industries case study provides a good example of a spokesperson who appears to lack a sense of empathy and seems oblivious to the plight of those impacted by the disruption to the water supply.

Approximately 7500 gallons of crude 4-Methylcyclohexanemethanol (MCHM) leaked from a one-inch hole in a Freedom Industries tank and made its way to the Elk River and down to the drinking water intake for 300,000 West Virginia residents. Within a day, the company – newly merged with three partners a week and a half prior – was facing numerous lawsuits. One week later, Freedom Industries filed for bankruptcy.

During media training, I often use a clip of company president Gary Southern's news conference as an example of what *not* to do.

Here's the real Gary Southern:

Fig. 2-7. A video clip of the real Gary Southern press conference can be found at
https://www.youtube.com/watch?v=hAGixCOj8bg

Despite the disruption to the community's water supply, Gary Southern thirstily swigged water throughout the press conference. He wandered off camera. And he tried to cut the press conference short when the going got tough. Worse, he allowed the media to lead him back for more flagellation. Southern's performance became the butt of parodies:

Fig. 2-8. Tom Hansen's parody of Gary Southern can be found at
https://www.youtube.com/watch?v=poU8V1ITP_0

Lesson learned: choose your spokespersons carefully and make sure they are well prepped. Gary Southern bumbled through the press conference without any apparent understanding of what to do or not and showed little empathy for the water crisis his company had caused.

2.3.2 Emerging Issues Crises

There are three main categories of crisis:

- Natural disaster.
- Man-made hazards or accidents by employees.
- Hazards originating outside the company which become a crisis for the company.

All of these are examples of "abrupt" crises with a defining point where the situation becomes an incident, emergency, disaster, or crisis.

"Emerging issues" are layered incidents which build to become a crisis. Contributing factors are overlooked and the patterns are often difficult to detect until the situation becomes a crisis. Organizations are constantly bombarded with information and when the "signal-to-noise ratio" is high, an organization may be distracted by the individual pieces rather than seeing the overall pattern.

How to detect:

- Keep attuned to what stakeholders are concerned about.
- What portions of your website are stakeholders most interested in?
- What issues are repeatedly being raised on social platforms?
- What angers public interest or pressure groups?

By keeping attuned to what stakeholders are concerned about, you can better forecast emerging issues for your organization – and take measures to ameliorate them *before* they become an emerging issues *crisis*.

2.3.3 "Trust Us" Only Works Once: Taco Bell's Emerging Issues Case Study (December 12, 2006)[20]

The public generally responds more favorably to organizations that show a human side and sincerely acknowledge messing up. Or at least they do the first time. Who hasn't made a mistake? Many people (including victims of the event) are often willing to give the benefit of the doubt to an organization that appears to be sincerely sorry for an error. But "trust us, it won't happen again" only works once. If the same thing happens a second time, the organization's credibility will be damaged and explanations and promises will be received skeptically.

Taco Bell found itself in the middle of an emerging issues crisis in December 2006 which continued to erupt and erode spokesperson attempts to reassure customers that Taco Bell was safe to eat.

2.3.3.1 The Initial Problem

- Hundreds of Taco Bell customers in five northeastern US states reported cases of food poisoning.
- Of the hundreds of reported cases, 64 cases were confirmed as *E. coli* poisoning. Each of the confirmed cases had eaten at Taco Bell.
- *E. coli* is a bacterium found in the gut of animals. It can cause bloody diarrhea and kidney failure. An estimated 73,000 cases of infection and 60 deaths in the US are caused each year by *E. coli.*
- Federal investigators report their prime suspect was green onions.
- Taco Bell removed green onions from its 5,982 restaurants in the US and Canada after a preliminary test of three samples found them to be "presumptive" positive.
- The three samples later turned out to be negative.
- Taco Bell then announced it would not return green onions to menus and that it had switched suppliers in the Northeast.
- *"Based on this testing and all that we know today, I can reassure you that all Taco Bell food is safe and strict standards are being upheld at all of our restaurants"* (Greg Creed, Taco Bell President).

Questions for Further Thought and Discussion

- ➢ *If you were part of the communications team for Taco Bell, what would you be communicating?*
- ➢ *What do you think about the decision to pull green onions off the menu?*

- Federal officials advise shredded lettuce was the most likely source of the Taco Bell *E. coli* outbreak.
- Although *E. coli* had not been found in samples of lettuce, officials pinpoint it as the likely source based on a statistical analysis of what patrons who became ill say they ate as compared with patrons who didn't get sick.
- The statistical analysis also indicated cheddar cheese and ground beef could also be the culprits but based on the history of outbreaks of food-borne illness associated with the three foods, lettuce is the most likely source, since beef is cooked and cheese is pasteurized.
- 70 percent of Taco Bell's menu items contain lettuce.
- The lettuce was supplied by Ready Pac, a California produce company.
- 71 Taco Bell customers had gotten *E. coli* so far. None died.
- Taco Bell executives continue to try to reassure customers it is safe to eat at Taco Bell.

Question for Further Thought and Discussion

➢ *If you were part of the communications team for Taco Bell, what would you say to reassure customers that it is safe to eat at Taco Bell?*

2.3.3.3 Three months later – (March 2007)[22]

- The Southern California farm that grew the green onions that were first linked to and then cleared in last year's *E. coli* outbreak filed a lawsuit against Taco Bell.
- They claim Taco Bell "engaged in an irresponsible and intentional crusade to save its own brand at the expense of an innocent supplier" … and cost the supplier millions of dollars of business.
- Taco Bell said in a statement that it was acting responsibly and was only trying to keep the public informed of developments.
- The incident cost Taco Bell $20 million so far.

- A dozen rats were caught on video scurrying across the floor of a NYC KFC/Taco Bell – running between counters and tables and climbing on children's highchairs.
- News crews flocked to the windows and by midmorning the footage was all over the Internet and TV news, with onlookers giving a play-by-play from the sidewalk as the rodents moved about.

Take a look:

Fig. 2-9. News coverage of NYC KFC/Taco Bell rat problem at
http://www.youtube.com/watch?v=su0U37w2tws

Questions for Further Thought and Discussion

➤ *We know what Taco Bell has been communicating about the food poisoning crisis, but what does this piece of information communicate about Taco Bell?*

➤ *As a consumer, how much would you trust the cleanliness and safety of Taco Bell's food at this point in time and what would it take to get you to change your mind?*

Lesson learned: "Trust us, it won't happen again" only works once. This can be especially tricky in emerging issues crises where multiple failures layer atop each other to step up the crisis for the organization. Taken singly, they might not have been as bad as the combined whole which underscored the quality assurance lapses and compromised credibility.

2.4 Additional Elements That Make Communication with the Media Effective

- **Build alliances**. Your official spokesperson is not necessarily going to be the most trusted person to those who have been impacted by a crisis. What s/he says is likely to be treated with a great deal of skepticism, because of course it is their job to cast the organization (and whatever the organization just did) in the best light possible.
- **Speak clearly and concisely**. Use simple language that is easily understood. Jargon obfuscates. Assume those covering your event are not experts in your industry. Make it simple for them to get the story right and they will be more likely to.
- **Think strategic and long-term.** Successful crisis response does not begin on the day of the crisis. Planning for crisis in advance will almost always lead to a more effective outcome than "winging it."
- **Listen to your audiences**. Are you communicating what *you* want your audiences to know or are you communicating what *they* want to know? Listen to the questions they have and create a dialog.

2.4.1 Official Spokespersons Aren't Always the Most Credible

As CNN aired video of US tanks rolling into Baghdad during the first Persian Gulf war in 1991, Iraqi spokesperson "Baghdad Bob" was quoted as saying "We have them surrounded in their tanks… They're not even [within] 100 miles [of Baghdad]. They are not in any place. They hold no place in Iraq. This is an illusion… they are trying to sell to the others an illusion."

Junior level employees are often seen as more trustworthy than official spokespersons or execs for this reason. [Consider whether you can empower them to talk to the press. More on this in section 10.8.] Even more trustworthy are unofficial spokespersons who the public sees as credible because they have nothing whatsoever to lose by backing you. Police and fire officials often fall into this category. Are there impartial respected experts in your community who could be added to your advisory or corrective actions team? Can you build a bridge in advance with the community surrounding your location(s)? What they have to say about having you as a neighbor can be much more meaningful than any words from your spokesperson. [See unsolicited letters following the Bristol tote spill in section 3.7.4.1.]

2.4.2 Case Study – Ford River Rouge (1999)

Although twenty years have passed, this case study remains an excellent example of the power of unofficial spokesperson testimonials.

On February 1, 1999 a massive explosion and fire at Ford's iconic River Rouge facility in Dearborn Michigan, killed several workers and injured dozens more. The unofficial spokespersons who stepped forward to add their accounts bolstered what the company had to say in a way that the official spokespersons could never have done as effectively.[23]

> **William Clay Ford:** You could argue that William Clay Ford Jr., Ford Motor's chairman and great grandson of Ford founder Henry Ford, was of course an official spokesperson, but his actions and the strain in his voice spoke louder and more credibly than his words. Within an hour of the explosion, as firefighters were still trying to put out the blaze, Ford arrived at the scene of the blast to check on employees.

> "It's awful," said Ford, dressed in an open-collar shirt sans suit jacket and tie, and who appeared visibly ashen and shaken. "Everyone who works at Ford is an extended member of the family. This is the worst day of my life."

> Ford later visited hospitals and spoke with victims' relatives. He had taken the reigns as Chairman only one month before.

> **Crystal Harper (widow of pipefitter Donald Harper who died in the blast):** "My family and I would like to express our gratitude for all the prayers, expressions of sympathy and the care

37

people have shown us. The [United Auto Workers union] and Ford Motor Co. have been extremely helpful during this time."

Union Vice President Ron Gettelfinger: Union officials applauded Ford's handling of the explosion, saying Ford put people above profits following the tragedy and thanked Edsel Ford II, a board member and great-grandson of founder Henry Ford, for attending an employee counseling session Tuesday morning. Edsel Ford II also attended several of the funerals.

"Ford Motor Co. has never raised the issue of production throughout this crisis," said Gettelfinger. "We've started discussion about getting the operations back. They have dealt with the human side of the story, and I want to applaud Ford Motor Co.," he said.

Lesson learned: unofficial spokespersons can be more credible and may be more trusted than your official spokesperson. Cultivate and harness unofficial advocates.

2.5 Tactics When You May Be to Blame

In the coffee shop example in Chapter 1, we talked about a crisis where the organization was a victim of circumstances rather than truly at fault. But if the crisis you are facing is the result of an accident your organization caused, there are additional tactics you may want to consider. Noted crisis expert Jim Lukaszewski developed the checklist below of things to take into account when developing a holistic response to this sort of crisis.

- **Explanation** – why did it happen and what did you learn?
- **Declaration** – public commitment and positive steps to be taken to resolve the situation.
- **Contrition** – continuing verbalization of regret, sympathy, embarrassment and acceptance of responsibility.
- **Consultation** – ask for help (from those most directly affected) to design solutions to preclude the situation from happening again.

- **Commitment** – publicly set goals at zero (zero errors, zero defects, zero dumb decisions, zero problems).
- **Restitution** – find a way to quickly pay the price. Go beyond expectations.[24]

The points Lukaszewski makes are important. Explain not only what happened but be humble enough to explain what you learned. This goes hand in hand with declaration and commitment. What are the steps you will take to right the errors (and the people impact of those errors)? Take those steps beyond simply explaining what you will do to fix the problem. Commit to putting in place measures to ensure the situation never happens again. Remember, this can't just be lip service; if the same thing happens again, you will lose all credibility and consumer and victim confidence in the value of your word.

2.5.1 Case Study in Commitment Backfiring – Chipotle (2015)

Repetitive failures are very damaging to reputation because they trigger a loss of confidence in the organization's ability to fix the problem and do the right thing without outside pressure forcing it to do so.

In 2015, Chipotle closed dozens of restaurants on the West Coast when health authorities linked the restaurant chain to an E. coli outbreak. A month later, more than 80 students in Boston were sickened. After its stock price lost about 30 percent of its value, CEO Steve Ells publicly declared improved safety standards that would make the fast food chain the "safest place to eat" from that point forward, but more sickness continued.[25]

Questions for Further Thought and Discussion

➢ *In the Chipotle case study above, what was the limit on Chipotle saying "trust us" we've fixed the problem?*
➢ *Why did their statement of commitment backfire?*
➢ *If you were in Chipotle's shoes when this was happening, what would you have done to arrive at a different outcome?*

Lesson learned: Promising no more failures, errors, accidents, problems can be an important tactic in demonstrating your commitment to fixing a problem. But if you don't actually fix the problem, the promise will ring hollow and you will lose all credibility.

2.5.2 Contrition

Contrition is a powerful incentive for gaining the forgiveness of those impacted. Do not underestimate the value of a genuine apology – not just lip service. Lawyers often don't want the company to accept responsibility or acknowledge fault for an accident because that could negatively impact chances of prevailing in the lawsuits to come. Work with your lawyers on finding a middle ground that they can accept. Apologies can deter lawsuits from being filed in the first place if they are unsolicited, quick and 100 percent sincere. [See chapter 8 on Apology.]

2.5.3 Consultation

Consultation is the tactic Starbucks used when it worked with the families of the employees who had been killed to identify a means to memorialize them. [See section 1.5.] Asking for those impacted to be part of the solution is the best way to gain buy-in for the solution(s). The key here is being willing to listen to and adapt suggestions brought forward, and to work collaboratively as partners to find a fix that is workable (from your end) and which they feel is a win for their end. You won't have to promote the identified solutions. They will be proud to talk about it!

2.5.4 Restitution Case Study – Tote Spill (June 2014)

Of all the solutions above, restitution is often the hardest to convince senior leadership – or the legal team – to enact but can also be the most powerful. As in the Ford case study earlier in this chapter, leaving stakeholders feeling that the organization puts "people above profits" can go a long way toward forgiveness and makes them less likely to sue for additional punitive damages. To be most effective, restitution should be an immediate righting or easing of hardship without waiting for a court to decide whether fault is yours to take and what the fair punishment should be. It is the equivalent of saying "we don't know who is at fault but that does not matter. We're taking these actions regardless because it is the right thing to do."

For example, rain and slippery conditions led to a tote (reusable plastic container for transporting chemicals) of ethyl acrylate falling off a forklift at the Arkema Bristol plant (outside of Philadelphia) in June 2014. Ethyl acrylate is a chemical used in the production of polymers including resins, plastics, and rubber. It is odiferous and a small amount of the product can be smelled for miles. In this case, the spill could be smelled offsite (all the way across the river to New Jersey). Nearby businesses closed and sent employees home because they did not know what they were smelling or whether it was dangerous. And the principal for the local elementary school decided to shelter-in-place students, despite the end-of-year "fun day" carnival taking place that day.

Because the plant manager had an existing relationship with nearby businesses (as a result of attendance at regular Community Advisory Panel meetings), he was able to call each nearby business to **explain** what happened and answer any questions they had.

Similarly, the business unit president reached out to the school's principal to not only offer an apology (**contrition**) for the scare and misunderstanding that caused a cancellation of the kids' fun, but to ask what he could do to help (**restitution**). The principal explained that the parent teacher organization had spent the year fund-raising for the event and the vendors needed to be paid despite the cancellation. The business unit president was on site the next day with a check for the full amount.

Mr. Papadourakis,

Thank you for your consideration and support for Mary Devine. Our students and their families are very grateful. We are fortunate to have Arkema as a neighbor.

Sincerely,
Brian Galloway, Principal
Mary Devine Elementary

The key here is not only doing the right thing but going one step beyond expectations.

Lesson learned: Going one step beyond what victims truly expect lessens anger and makes those impacted less likely to hold a grudge. In some (albeit rare) cases, it can even turn injured parties into advocates.

Summary

Social media dynamics play a substantial role in crisis communication today. Even traditional media have embraced the use of social media. This chapter covered the most critical elements that make crisis communications effective as well as the tactics you can consider for crises where your organization may be to blame.

Questions for Further Thought and Discussion

➢ *Have you encountered a situation where the restitution tactic could have been employed? If you had it to do over again, what would you have done differently and what do you think the effect would have been?*

➢ *What would it have cost to employ the restitution tactic in that situation, vs. what it actually cost (all costs included)?*

CHAPTER 3

WHO TRUSTS A CHEMICAL COMPANY?

At Arkema, their neighbors do – as a result of the crisis strategies I helped them put in place. This includes being up front with the hardest of news, rather than waiting and hoping it will go unnoticed.

This chapter covers:

- *An in-depth analysis of Arkema's 2017 crisis at Crosby, Texas following Hurricane Harvey, including the crisis strategies the author put in place in the years leading up to the crisis.*
- *Initial steps.*
- *Spokesperson performance.*
- *Community relations.*
- *Darksite strategy.*
- *Breaking the story first.*
- *Being a good neighbor.*
- *Thinking long term and strategic.*

When Hurricane Harvey left Arkema's Crosby TX chemical plant under six feet of water in August 2017, Arkema's CEO called a press conference to publicly and unequivocally state that the plant would explode and that all neighbors needed to evacuate. Emergency responders were sent to every home within a 1.5-mile radius to ensure those at risk were made aware. A toll-free hotline (established years before) was activated. Arkema sent its "go team" to the site to work with each neighbor to make sure all their needs were taken care of.

Similarly, Arkema's social media tools have been dedicated to focus primarily on volunteerism (rather than marketing) within the small communities surrounding each plant. It was a calculated strategy I put in place to emphasize the role that Arkema employees play as members of each of those communities: judging science fairs, holding blood drives, building houses, cleaning creeks. I banked on the fact that the media would go to these online sources to find more information following a crisis. (I worked for many years as a television news producer. When something explodes, it's going to make the news. When an event fails to occur on schedule, other material must fill the time. If you can get people to say awful things, that makes for good news clips. If people have nothing to say but nice things, it makes for a more involved and interesting story – everyone expects neighbors to say that chemical companies are bad neighbors. When they say the opposite, it turns heads.)

My strategy worked. Following the Crosby crisis, negative postings were loudly shouted down with unsolicited comments from an organic up-swelling from communities bearing witness to Arkema as a good neighbor, not a bad one. Here is a more in-depth look.

3.1 Arkema's Crisis at Crosby TX (2017)

No successful crisis response begins on the day of the crisis.

To the east of Houston, Arkema's Crosby plant is relatively small, with approximately 55 people tending organic peroxides. Organic peroxides require refrigeration to keep them stable. Its neighbors are few, keep to themselves and have little interaction with the plant.

As Hurricane Harvey approached and later as it began walloping Houston on August 25, 2017, Arkema's Crosby's "ride-out crew" (the minimal number of people needed to tend the plant in a disaster) shut down operations and secured the most volatile of its temperature-sensitive material in several trailers parked on the plant's highest ground with multiple layers of protection before evacuating. It wasn't enough.

The storm battered Houston and flooded the plant with six feet of water, and the layers of protection designed to keep the organic peroxide refrigerated fell away.

Arkema contacted Harris County (a massive county that surrounds Houston) emergency responders and explained that the organic peroxide which the company was monitoring remotely had lost refrigeration and was coming up to ambient temperature. Fire and spontaneous combustion were inevitable. The plant, as well as the surrounding area, needed to be completely evacuated.

A company without scruples could have looked at the distance between the plant and its nearest neighbors and decided that it was worth the risk to business and reputation to keep quiet and do nothing but wait for the explosion. Announcing an impending explosion would draw enormous attention to the company, and lots of reporters would look for dirt. There are companies that would calculate that the risk was worth taking. In fact, dozens of chemical plants in the Houston area, released more than one million pounds of carcinogens into the atmosphere and more than five million pounds of toxins into the floodwaters following Hurricane Harvey, and not a single one of them announced their accidents to the communities or media.

Instead of following suit, Rich Rowe, CEO of Arkema's North American operations, held a press conference Wednesday, August 30th to announce that the material could not be re-stabilized. Arkema, therefore, in coordination with the county's emergency managers, planned to allow the material to disintegrate, which would likely result in the plant exploding within the next several hours or days.

5:55 PM EDT, August 30, 2017
The nation is dealing with a natural disaster of enormous magnitude in Texas. As part of that, Arkema is dealing with a critical issue at our Crosby, Texas, facility…

Our Crosby facility makes organic peroxides, a family of compounds that are used in everything from making pharmaceuticals to construction materials. But organic peroxides may burn if not stored and handled under the right conditions. At Crosby, we prepared for what we recognized could be a worst-case scenario. We had redundant contingency plans in place. Right now, we have an unprecedented six feet of water at the plant. We have lost primary power and two sources of emergency backup power. As a result, we have lost critical refrigeration of the materials on site that could now explode and cause a subsequent intense fire. The high water and lack of power leave us with no way to prevent it. We have evacuated our personnel for their own safety. The federal, state and local authorities were contacted a few days ago, and we are working very closely with them to manage this matter. They have ordered the surrounding community to be evacuated, too…

3.2 The Tier II Report

In the Fall of 2015, The Houston Chronicle's investigative team had begun running a multi-part series castigating lax self-oversight of the chemical industry, especially in Texas.[26]

Arkema was among the companies targeted, but reporting was flawed. Temperature-sensitive organic peroxides are volatile without refrigeration, but their danger is the risk of explosion, not toxicity. Once ignited, organic peroxides will burn vigorously and will be difficult to extinguish. If a peroxide is heated above a certain temperature, the rate of decomposition (fire or explosion) will increase in an uncontrolled manner.[27]

The misunderstanding led the media to conclude the smoke from the fire that burned two years later following the Crosby explosion August 31 was toxic.

3.3 Initial Community Response Steps

As expected, at approximately 2:00 am Thursday August 31, the organic peroxide in one of the trailers reached ambient temperature, spontaneously combusted, and melted down into the floodwaters leaving behind not much beyond soot. Witnesses heard "popping" noises as the pressurized container released. The media played an endless loop showing the container burning.

Fig. 3-1. Video coverage from the fire at Crosby can be found at
https://www.cnn.com/videos/us/2017/09/02/fires-chemical-plant-texas-todd-sot.cnn

Although a sheriff's deputy and more than a dozen first responders attempting to hold the 1.5-mile perimeter were taken to the hospital for examination and observation, all were subsequently released later in the morning.

3.4 Spokesperson Performance

In addition to media-training all of the plant managers at Arkema, with multiple on-site backups, we recognized years ago that any on-site personnel would likely have their hands full in the early stages of an emergency. All business unit leaders were media-trained as well so that even a leader from an aligned business unit could step in if necessary to take some of the burden off of the plant manager. Of the potential cadre of senior leaders I trained, Daryl Roberts rose to the top because of his ability to show empathy in his face in a way that is unquestionably sincere and believable. But business unit President Rich Rennard was the first to get on-scene from King of Prussia, Pennsylvania headquarters. He held a press conference the morning of the first fire.

3.4.1 Arkema Chemical Plant Press Conference Transcript[28]

RICH RENNARD, ARKEMA EXECUTIVE, TEXAS: You have smoke, and any smoke is going to be an irritant to your eyes, your lungs or potentially your skin. So, if you're exposed to that, we're encouraging anyone that may be exposed to smoke coming from this fire, to contact their doctor or to seek medical advice.
QUESTION. A campfire, is that correct?
RENNARD: I heard the sheriff say that, and the Chief say that. I don't want to necessarily compare the intensity of the smoke of this ...
QUESTION: I heard the sheriff say this is no more dangerous than a barbeque.
RENNARD: I heard the comment but again I don't want to make any kind of comparisons on the kind of smoke that's coming from our fire.
QUESTION: So, you can't be sure that it's just a campfire smoke, you can't be sure that it's ...

RENNARD: No, but I can tell you the toxicity from the smoke will certainly cause an irritation to your eyes, and irritation to your lungs, just like any smoke. We encourage not to – to avoid getting exposed to that.

QUESTION: People want to know how in danger they are.

RENNARD: So, with the recommendation from local authorities we've established this one-and-a-half-mile evacuation zone. We believe along with the local authorities that we've moved everyone out of harm's way, and that no one is in danger based on the fire that we expect... We're not going to put anyone in harm's way to restore refrigeration, because we don't know the state of the product in the containers... If they exceed a certain temperature, they begin to decompose, and that decomposition process generates the heat, and ultimately produces the fire.

QUESTION: What is the possibility that one of the explosions could rupture other chemicals on site?

RENNARD: As I said, the containers are remote enough, we don't anticipate damage to other property on site.

QUESTION: If you said the chemicals could burn, is there any potential for them not to burn and release into floodwaters and if so, do damage?

RENNARD: No. We anticipate the products will decompose once they warm up and burn.

QUESTION: Can you say the fumes are not toxic?

RENNARD: The toxicity of the fumes? You mean the smoke?

QUESTION: Yes.

RENNARD: I don't know the composition of the smoke...

QUESTION: You are not able to say any of this is non-toxic?

RENNARD: Organic peroxides are, as the Sheriff said, they are chemical materials used to initiate other chemical production for the purpose of making plastics. Toxicity is a –

QUESTION: You are not going to say they are non-toxic correct? Are you going to say they are or not? Yes, or no? I think it's a pretty important question.

RENNARD: The smoke is noxious. It's relative. If you breathe in the smoke, it's going to irritate your lungs...

49

QUESTION: It's not going to kill you?
RENNARD: No. We don't believe that to be the case.

QUESTION: After this is done, should people around here be comfortable having Arkema as a neighbor?
RENNARD: I think so. We have been responding to this the best we can. We have set up a hotline for people who have experienced issues related to this. And a claims line as well. So, we encourage people, if they have been – if they have injuries or damage to their property as a result of our issue to call the hotline.
QUESTION: Can you share that number?...

3.4.2 Armchair Quarterbacking Rich Rennard's Press Conference

---

Rich,

Good job. You remained very calm and looked relaxed. Open collar shirt was a good choice. Glasses off so people could see your eyes, rather than reflection, was on target.

Next time give your title as "Arkema spokesperson". Your actual full title is less important (and may leave reporters wondering why someone aligned with the BU wasn't the one to talk.

I believe the hotline is 877-4-ARKEMA (and make clear that we have already begun to assist those impacted, (if that is the case)).

Get some technical experts ready to jump in when you call on them. People were left feeling a little bit like you didn't understand the tech issues. I saw you try to refer questions to your off-camera backers a couple of times but the camera never widened out enough to see them. Whoever was behind you needs to be prepared to step up next time – with easy to understand explanation of what we expect to happen (i.e. fire/explosion within the contained parameter (don't let them say "decomposition" instead of explosion)... no expected risk from other chemicals nor from organic peroxides in the smoke, that the liquid organic peroxides will not contaminate the environment...

Overall, though, you did well.

My thoughts are with you. Please let me know if there is anything I can do to help.

Regards,
Jo

Figure 1Fig. 3-2. Text of email sent to Rich Rennard following his press conference.

CROSBY, TX

RICHARD RENNARD
ARKEMA EXECUTIVE

CBSN

Fig. 3-3. Video of Rich Rennard answering media questions the day of the first explosion can be found at https://www.youtube.com/watch?v=zs5cExp-OFA

During media training, these were some of the things I coached Arkema spokespersons to do or not do and which Rich Rennard encountered during his press conference August 31:

- **Reporters want to see your eyes.** They believe they can judge whether you are trustworthy. Do not wear sunglasses. Unless you have non-reflective glasses, remove them. (I never coached Rich Rennard to put his glasses on top of his head – that was a little odd. But at least he remembered to remove them!)

- **Don't wear a suit.** Roll up your sleeves. (Rich Rennard wore an open-collared shirt which made him look like he was there to get down to work rather than a stuffed shirt sent in from corporate to "handle" the statement.)

- **Have a wingman ready to jump in** with the technical details in case you hit a question you don't know the answer to. (Although the cameras never widened out enough to see them, on a couple of occasions during the press conference, viewers can see Rich Rennard attempt to refer questions to off-camera backers. The technical experts standing off camera could have done a better job jumping in to assist on those occasions with easy to understand explanations.)

- **If asked about medical consequences or impacts to people, mention the hotline** we've created and emphasize that we will take care of them.

3.4.3 Two Questions Continue to Surface

Rich Rennard was unflappable as he faced the crush of reporters the morning of August 31. He did a good job handling very difficult questions; but two continued to surface because he (and CEO Rich Rowe in his press conference a day earlier) still weren't getting the words out clearly enough.

1. Is the smoke toxic?
2. Will you release the Tier II report? (Tier II reports—or Emergency and Hazardous Chemical Inventory Forms—are submitted annually to local fire departments, Local Emergency Planning Committees (LEPCs) and State Emergency Response Commissions (SERCs) to help those agencies plan for and respond to chemical emergencies.)

In the third press conference, CEO Rich Rowe read a carefully crafted statement designed to address the Tier II issue satisfactorily, and his expert wingman, VP of Manufacturing Daryl Roberts stood by to help handle some of the tough questions:

> Rich Rowe: *"Why won't we share our Tier II inventory? We understand that the public is worried. We know that everyone wants information and we respect that it is the public's right to have access to information. Our overriding concern… is to keep the public safe…*
>
> *As of this morning, we've posted on our website the names of the chemicals that we have at Crosby. We know, I know, that this is not the same as posting the Tier II reports. And there are good reasons for that. To state the obvious, we have dangerous chemicals at the Crosby site. We want to give the information that the public needs to feel and be safe. But we need to keep the more*

detailed information, for example, the precise quantity and the location of these chemicals from those that would do us harm. That said, we've shared every detail of our Tier II inventory with the people who are responsible for making decisions about public safety. Those are the federal, state, and local emergency response teams, and that led to the imposition of the 1.5-mile evacuation radius which Arkema fully supports."

"Secondly, why won't we share our RMP [risk management plan] for Crosby? Like the Tier II data, we recognize people are worried and want information. We've shared what we have with those that need the information to keep the public safe, and I'll say it once more: every decision we are making, every decision we make going forward is focused on keeping people safe. The RMP reports don't address the situation we have here. Organic peroxides are not regulated under the RMP regulations and therefore are not included in the RMP report. The situation we're facing at Crosby as a result of Hurricane Harvey is because organic peroxides became unstable because of the flooding and loss of power and, as a result, are increasing in temperature and becoming increasingly unstable. The chemicals that require the RMP report for Crosby are sulfur dioxide and isoamylase. These substances are located onsite in tanks that were secured during the plant shutdown. The organic peroxides are located away from these storage tanks. RMP plans used to be publicly available. The regulations were changed to balance the public's right to know with the public's right to be secure. The balance between these two strong interests were set after considerable public debate. We're providing federal, state and local responders with the information they need to make decisions on facts as they exist today and that's what resulted in the 1.5-mile evacuation zone."

"Thirdly, is smoke from the fire toxic? Like smoke from any fire, smoke from organic peroxide fires can irritate the eyes, the nose, the lungs. And the smoke from these fires may also contain organic peroxide degradation products including hydrocarbons

and various alcohols, which also can irritate the eyes, skin, the respiratory system, create nausea, drowsiness, etc. Based on our understanding of the situation, we believe that these are the key health effects of the fires coming at Crosby. And for this reason we continue to advise everyone to avoid the smoke and seek medical attention if they are exposed."

Matt Dempsey, Houston Chronicle: *Did Arkema have the ability to neutralize the organic peroxides before this incident occurred?*

Daryl Roberts, VP Manufacturing: *"Having a neutralizing agent might be something that would be practical if we had a large volume of material that was in one tank.... But that's not the situation that we have here. What we have here is... all in containers that are in the range of a gallon jug up to a four- or five-gallon container so we're talking in the range of 10-15,000 individual small containers that are all palletized in boxes stacked in pallets in multiple locations. So the ability to try to neutralize all of that material during the hurricane... was to me just not a practical solution... With that much water that very likely would have led to leaks or spills which likely would have led to material leaving the site. So our strategy was to continue to keep this material in buildings or trailers where it was refrigerated. Unfortunately the water rose to the level that was higher than anyone had ever seen."*

Matt Dempsey: *How far in feet are the other chemicals from the organic peroxides, specifically the sulfur dioxide and isobutylene [sic]?*

Daryl Roberts: *"I don't have the exact number. The two chemicals I think that you are referencing are the RMP [risk management plan] chemicals?"*

Matt Dempsey: *"Yeah, your worst-case scenario."*

Roberts: *"Isoamylene is near the front of the plant. These [organic peroxide] materials are near the backside of the plant.*

SO2 [sulfur dioxide] is somewhat in the middle. So I would say it would be hundreds of yards and significantly more than that for isoamylene."

Matt Dempsey: *"Do you have any idea of the condition of the containers for those two materials?"*

Roberts: *"At this point from everything we've seen from the aerial, there's been no issues related to any of those materials. There's been no fire that's impinged on any or any water damage. We see no degradation in any of the systems around the RMP chemicals that you're asking about."*

Dempsey: *If you can tell us the components of your Tier II chemicals, why can't you just tell us what they are and the quantities?*

Roberts: *"On the website we have posted exactly what they are. The full list of our Tier II chemicals has been posted. The only information that we have not posted is the exact amount and locations within the site. And if you think about the reasons why the decision was made to make some of that information confidential, it was for security reasons from a terrorism standpoint, so we do not want to take the step of providing exact volumes and pinpoint exactly where those things are on the site. That was a policy that was established from a regulatory standpoint and I'll let the regulators take the lead on if they want to change that policy but we don't want to take the lead of making a decision for them."*

Q: [ABC] *"I didn't seem to get a straight answer on this but the smoke that is burning, obviously you guys have said it is an irritant, not to be around it, if you've been exposed to it, seek medical attention. But is it toxic?"*

Roberts: *"I think we've told you what the health effects are. They are all acute health effects... I'm not sure how to answer that question other than to say we know the health effects are having a sore throat, or cough, or what you would see with any other type of smoke is what you can expect. I'll let you determine how you want to describe that or classify it. Clearly we won't say that there are no health effects because any time you are impacted by smoke there is an impact on the body. We would expect individuals to stay away from that environment if they see it. We would expect people to stay out of that mile and a half range."*

In a press conference September 4th, Rich Rennard again addressed the issue of toxicity. This time, his explanation was even clearer and was delivered in a way that finally made sense to the layperson. Rather than dancing around the issue of toxicity for several days, Arkema should have explained from the beginning that the organic peroxides left little – if any – residue behind when they burned, it was the *trailers* that released plastic and rubber toxins as they melted.

> Reporter: *You talked about air quality testing… is there potential for what has burned to settle in water, on the ground, or stuff like that. Long-term damage?*
>
> Rich Rennard: *So certainly this was a fire. And with any fire there is ash and that ash is ultimately going to fall out of the sky and land on the ground. So what we're doing, and instructing residents to do is, if they see any debris or ash that falls under their property, we would encourage them to call our hotline, and then we will send a team of people out to remove that debris from their property.*
>
> Reporter: *Should they consider that ash to be more dangerous than something from a campfire or normal fire?*
>
> Rich Rennard: *It's debris that would be similar to a house fire… When these materials were burning they were inside these trailers and the trailers were made out of… materials. The product was packaged in plastic so there's going to be plastic, trailers, and rubber tires on them. Those tires burned. There's insulation on the inside of the trailers, that burn. So that's the kind of combustible materials that would typically be found in that kind of ash.*

3.5 Community Relations Through Online and Social Media

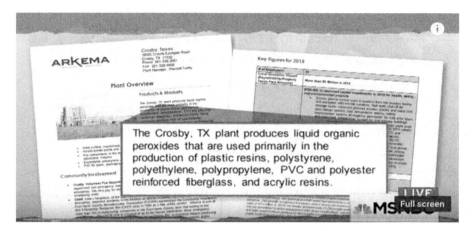

Fig. 3-4. Screen grab from a Rachel Maddow MSNBC broadcast showing Arkema's one-page overview on Crosby verbatim. https://www.youtube.com/watch?v=_UvL-io4KWk

Investment in health, environment and safety	$700,000 in approved capital investments in 2015 for health, safety, and environmental projects
	• Crosby plant's control room is isolated from the process facility and equipped with remote cameras, high level shut off for storage tanks, restricted process access, reactor and wash tank auto deluge system, high temperature alarms, safety instrumented system, emergency generators for safe shut down, and redundant refrigeration system for cold storage buildings.
	○ Air pollution control equipment at the Crosby plant uses state of the art technology, meeting the US EPA criteria for best available control technology (BACT) and considerably reduces emissions from the facility, allowing the plant to achieve greater than 99.5%+ destruction of VOCs (Volatile Organic Compounds), while scrubbers remove 99%+ of SO_2 and acid gases.
	• Part of Responsible Care, an industry-wide initiative among members of the American Chemistry Council to demonstrate continuing commitment to health, safety and the environment.
	○ Created an innovative program for customers to return empty organic peroxide containers for recycling, reducing landfill use and associated fees.
Safety record	One lost-time injury in the last 7 years

Figure3-5. Detail from the publicly available one-page overview for Crosby. https://www.arkema-americas.com/export/sites/americas/.content/medias/downloads/arkema-in-the-americas/arkema-inc-crosby-texas-site-overview-2017.pdf

3.5.1 First, Make Good News Easy to Find

The community relations strategy at Arkema included having positive information easily available for the media to find. Despite being France's largest chemical company, most people in the US had never heard of Arkema, so we knew that in a crisis, one of the first things they'd do is search for more information.

The Arkema Americas website (https://www.arkema-americas.com/en/arkema-americas/) lists each plant alphabetically down its left side. Clicking the name of any of the plants brings up a simple one-page overview with contact information, photos, a paragraph or two about the products produced at that plant, a table itemizing the plant's safety record, safety precautions, and community sponsorships. The "one-pagers" also have a "community news" item showcasing at least one example of community interaction or assistance from within the last year. The effect is intended to provide a positive snapshot and position Arkema as a good neighbor, so that when the media searched during a crisis, it would be the first thing they'd find.

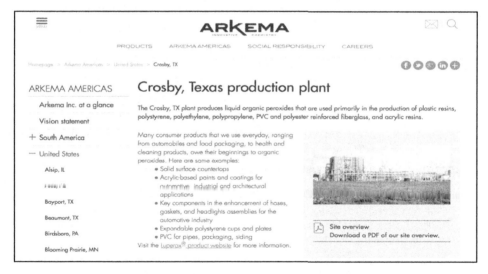

Fig. 3-6. Detail from the Arkema Crosby plant one-pager available online during the crisis. Current one-pagers for each site can be found at https://www.arkema-americas.com/en/arkema-americas/united-states/

Calvert City, KY

Cary, NC

Chatham, VA

Chester, SC

Clear Lake, TX

Crosby, TX

Exton, PA

Franklin, VA

Geneseo, NY

Grand Rapids, MI

Houston, TX

King of Prussia, PA - Headquarters

Louisville, KY

Memphis, TN

North Kansas City, MO

Pineville, LA

St. Charles, LA

Community involvement

- Crosby Volunteer Fire Department – We host annual drills in coordination with the local fire department and emergency medical team to coordinate likely interaction in the event of an emergency. We also pay for local fire department to attend fire training with plant emergency team.
- CAER Line – Neighbors of the plant are encouraged to call the CAER line for information about emergency response incidents in the facilities or off-site incidents that may impact the community. East Harris County Manufacturers Association (ECHMA) established the Community Awareness and Emergency Response line (CAER Line) in 1986 as a free public service. Arkema is one of more than 125 manufacturing companies in the East Harris County area that belong to the organization. The CAER Line is a source of up to the minute information about emergency response actions that are underway, involving an explosion, fire, or chemical release producing smoke, fumes, odors or noise that the public can see, smell, or hear, or may require public protective actions (such as evacuation or shelter-in-place).
- Arkema also utilizes, **EMerge Systems**, a web based multi-media communication tool used to communicate plant emergencies to local authorities. Activation occurs via a 24-hour manned website. Harris County Homeland

Community news

Jump Rope For Heart

Arkema's Crosby, Texas site partnered with the local Barrett Primary School to help support its "Jump Rope for Heart" event, which raised money for the American Heart Association®. Donations will help children who are born with "special hearts" live a happier, healthier lifestyle. The Crosby site donated juice and cookies for over 800 students to help them fuel up and cool off in between jump rope contests.

To learn more about Jump Rope for Heart, click here.

Fig. 3-7. Detail from the Arkema Crosby plant one-pager focusing on community involvement and available online at www.arkema-americas.com during the crisis.

3.5.2 Gearing Social Media to Focus on Community Ties

Social media also features prominently in Arkema's community relations strategy and similarly relies on an expectation that in the event of an explosion or chemical release, the media would check out Arkema's feeds to glean a broader understanding not only of the company's position, but also what kind of company Arkema is and what values it holds.

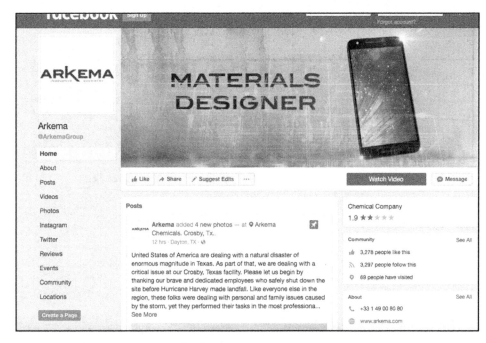

Fig. 3-8. Detail from Arkema's Facebook page during the crisis.

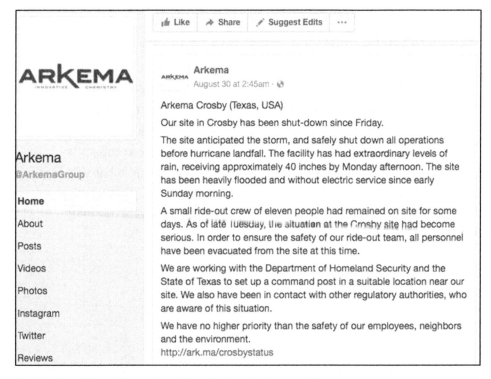

Fig. 3-9. Detail from Arkema's social media sites during the crisis.

Fig. 3-10. Detail from Arkema's social media sites during the crisis.

Community relations figures prominently here as well. Scroll deeper down Arkema's Facebook and Twitter pages, and you will find the sites filled with images and shout-outs about the strong ties Arkema's plants have with their communities.

Arkema Inc. added 4 new photos to the album: Houston, Texas Participates In Science Teachers Program — in ⚲ Houston, Texas.

August 11 at 9:05am · 🌐

This year marked the 21st year that Arkema's Houston, Texas site (http://ark.ma/Houston) participated in the company's annual Science Teachers Program. The program aims to help teachers uncover new ways to make science exciting for students. This year the plant hosted teachers from Cloverleaf Elementary. Teachers Abigail Marayag and Amalia Torres worked alongside Arkema mentor Luis Gonzalez to present a hands-on science kit and in-depth curriculum on the sun, moon and planet earth. Arkema purchased a science kit for the classroom, provided $500 to participating teachers and a donation to the school to replenish kit materials and additional science resources.

Fig. 3-11. Detail from Arkema's social media feeds in the weeks before the crisis.

64

Arkema Inc.
August 7 · 🌐

The West Chester, Pa. Sartomer site (http://ark.ma/WestChester) hosted a Community Action Panel (CAP) meeting in July. The CAP allows members to hear about the plant's operations and ask questions or raise concerns. It is one of the many ways that Arkema's Common Ground® Initiative meets its commitments and focuses on building relationships with stakeholders through communication and exchange. Three Sartomer employees and nine community members participated in the meeting. The community presented a recognition gift to former Plant Manager Ken Sweeney.

👍 Like   💬 Comment

Catherine Wallace, David V. Price, Kim Thompson Knotts and 11 others like this.

Fig. 3-12. Detail from Arkema's social media feeds in the weeks before the crisis.

Arkema Inc. added 3 new photos to the album: Axis, Ala.
Creola SAIL Center Luncheon — in ◉ Creola, Alabama.
August 4 · 🌐

Arkema's Axis, Ala. Service Team (http://ark.ma/Axis) and members of
management spent time at the Creola SAIL Center, an assisted living
facility that includes a senior community and provides services for
Alzheimer's care. This is the 10th year that the Axis plant provided a fun-
filled day for residents and staff. Arkema employees spent quality time with
the seniors, playing bingo and listening to music. The meals were
generously provided by Ron Prater's Catering.

👍 Like   💬 Comment

Catherine Wallace, David V. Price, Steve Lolli and 6 others like this.

Fig. 3-13. Detail from Arkema's social media feeds in the weeks before the crisis.

Arkema Inc. added 2 new photos.

July 6 · 🌐

Employees from Arkema's Axis, Ala. (Mobile) plant participated in United Way's annual "Day of Caring." Once a year, volunteers complete projects in their community that agencies don't otherwise have the money, staff or time to address. Arkema volunteers painted a wheel chair ramp, installed "no skid" strips, repaired and cleaned around picnic tables and made improvements to a pool table in a recreation area. Thank you to those who helped make a difference in our community!

To learn more about the Axis plant, visit: http://ark.ma/axis.

Fig. 3-14. Detail from Arkema's social media feeds in the weeks before the crisis.

3.5.3 The Community Reaction

In the hours following the initial explosion, angry comments intermixed with information about the response on Arkema's social media platforms. Arkema's tiny communications team couldn't keep up and allowed the negative comments to run unchallenged.

Michelle J. @zie42268
Replying to @Arkema_group@Arkema_Inc

I don't think this Richard guy was the correct person for this news conference.... Are your chemicals toxic or not?

Irma Gonzalez @RealCapricorn01

Why won't you release chemical inventory? Our lives are in danger, don't you care?

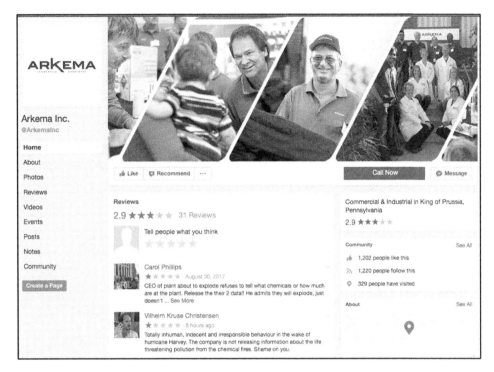

Fig. 3.15. Negative comments on Arkema's Twitter feed during the crisis.

But then an interesting thing began to happen. Intermixed alongside the angry comments, community members who had been touched by Arkema's efforts over the years spoke up. The organic welling up of support and affirmation was the ultimate demonstration of the effectiveness of the strategy I helped Arkema put in place years earlier.

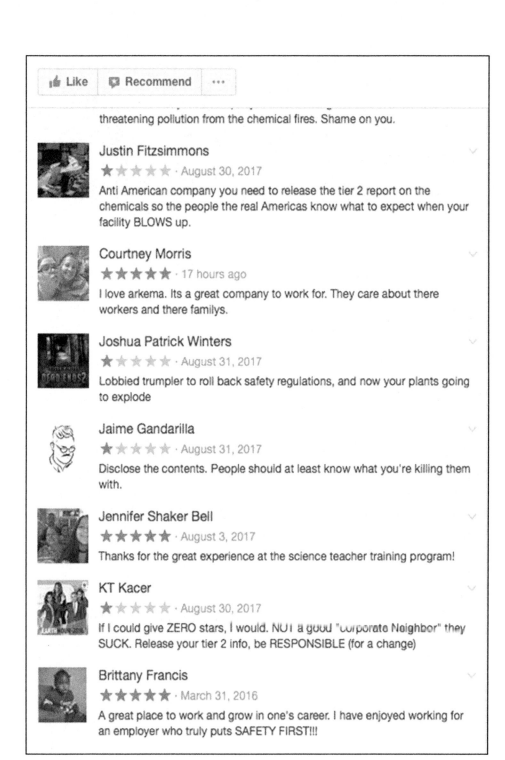

Justin Fitzsimmons
★ ★ ★ ★ ★ · August 30, 2017

Anti American company you need to release the tier 2 report on the chemicals so the people the real Americas know what to expect when your facility BLOWS up.

Courtney Morris
★ ★ ★ ★ ★ · 17 hours ago

I love arkema. Its a great company to work for. They care about there workers and there familys.

Joshua Patrick Winters
★ ★ ★ ★ ★ · August 31, 2017

Lobbied trumpler to roll back safety regulations, and now your plants going to explode

Jaime Gandarilla
★ ★ ★ ★ ★ · August 31, 2017

Disclose the contents. People should at least know what you're killing them with.

Jennifer Shaker Bell
★ ★ ★ ★ ★ · August 3, 2017

Thanks for the great experience at the science teacher training program!

KT Kacer
★ ★ ★ ★ ★ · August 30, 2017

If I could give ZERO stars, I would. NOT a good "corporate Neighbor" they SUCK. Release your tier 2 info, be RESPONSIBLE (for a change)

Brittany Francis
★ ★ ★ ★ ★ · March 31, 2016

A great place to work and grow in one's career. I have enjoyed working for an employer who truly puts SAFETY FIRST!!!

Fig. 3-16. Positive comments gain traction on Arkema's Twitter feed during the crisis.

3.6 Darksite Strategy

In the years before the Crosby crisis, I worked with the Arkema communications team to develop a workable darksite strategy that we could quickly and effectively employ with our minimal communications resources. In the event of a crisis, a darksite is a separate web site that has been continuously maintained so that it can go live to replace the organization's website with crisis-related information. Rather than mirroring the entire website with a "just in case" dark site, we developed and hid from public view until necessary, several template pages. We chose this simplified darksite strategy because we felt it would be absolutely necessary to acknowledge any crisis without burying the search for information in any way, *but* we also felt it was important not to overhaul the website completely and throw off those who came seeking non-crisis information. Our dark site strategy had to do both.

At the top of Arkema's main America's website, (https://www.arkema-americas.com/en/arkema-americas/) there is a scrolling carousel with approximately three banners that constantly rotate. Just below that are several smaller banners that remain stable. If a relatively minor incident were to happen, we planned to replace the first of the small banners with a picture signifying a red emergency beacon and an "Incident at ____ site" headline.

If a major incident or crisis were to happen, we planned to replace one of the major banners in the constantly scrolling carousel at the top of the homepage. Everything else on the homepage would stay in its original position.

In both cases, clicking on the identified banner or "learn more about the situation here" would take the user to the incident news page.

Nothing else about the website changed so that those who came searching for something else would be able to easily locate it and those who came searching for crisis information could easily be redirected to the one-pager for the site or the latest information and news.

Arkema justified not making statements and crisis information endlessly available. *("News posted here is for the sole purpose of informing the public of any current and/or ongoing incidents. Once the incident is resolved, this content will be replaced.")* It's of course bad form to remove social media posts because to do so looks like a cover up. Is it less genuine to clearly state an intention to freshen posts on an ongoing basis? Your web site, unless you have it on a platform like Facebook, which is unwise, is not social media. Changing the content – deleting pages, replacing pages – is par for the course.

Figure 3.17 shows what the Arkema homepage looked like when the Crosby event occurred and the darksite strategy was implemented.

Fig. 3-17. Screen grab of Arkema's homepage during the crisis.

Clicking on the banner took the reader to this page:

Fig. 3-18. Screen grab of the incident page during the crisis.

And this webpage:

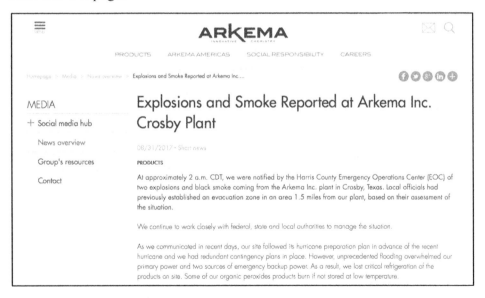

Fig. 3-19. Screenshot of statement detail available on Arkema's darksite incident page during the crisis.

3.7 Who Trusts a Chemical Company? – What Arkema Did Right

As mentioned in the beginning of this chapter, trust isn't something an organization can ask for, it's something they earn. "Bad" organizations – or those seen as not necessarily having the public's interest at heart – have an uphill battle earning trust because of innate skepticism.

The risk of chemical companies having an accident that causes injury is actually far below the average for other industries.

In 2016, the total recordable incident rate for the chemical industry as a whole was 2.0 incidents per 100 full time workers. Compare that to the US national average of 3.2 incidents per 100 full time workers. Industries you wouldn't assume to be more dangerous than chemical manufacturing come in significantly higher – grocery stores (4.3), chocolate manufacturing (4.4), hospitals (5.9), beet sugar manufacturing (8.5), veterinary services (12.3) Maybe you *would* expect veterinary services to come in high, but did you realize it was that much higher than chemical manufacturing? Even administrative and support services (2.2) has a higher rate of injuries than chemical manufacturing.[29]

Table 3-1. Total Reportable Cases Per 100 Full Time Workers (2016)

INDUSTRY	TOTAL REPORTABLE CASES PER 100 FULL TIME WORKERS (2016)
Chemical manufacturing	2.0
Administrative and support services	2.2
US National average	3.2
Grocery stores	4.3
Chocolate manufacturing	4.4
Hospitals	5.9
Beet sugar manufacturing	8.5
Veterinary services	12.3

On the surface that may seem hard to believe, but it is actually quite deliberate on the part of the chemical industry. That's because even the slightest accident may not only have serious consequences, including serious injury and death, but small accidents caused by carelessness, inattention, complacence, etc. may also be indicative of larger behavioral problems which in turn can signal a stronger likelihood of major accidents to come.

On the other hand, industries inherently deemed to be "safe" don't take the same precautions or have the same safety culture mindset. They don't necessarily hold mandatory monthly safety meetings focused on taking a good hard look at themselves and how they can constantly and continuously improve their safety record the way many chemical companies do.

Because chemical accidents can have nasty off-site impacts for neighbors, chemical companies are easy to lump into the "bad" neighbor category. But that wasn't the case with Arkema before the Crosby crisis of 2017. In fact, Arkema's 2016 total recordable injury rate was 1.5 – quite a bit lower than the average for the chemical industry.[30]

3.7.1 Breaking the Story First

When Hurricane Harvey flooded Arkema's Crosby Texas plant with six feet of water, precautions designed to keep onsite organic peroxides refrigerated failed. Once the unstable and temperature-sensitive organic peroxides reached the temperature of the outside air, Arkema management knew fire and spontaneous combustion were inevitable.

But they did not wait and hope. Instead, Arkema CEO Rich Rowe held a press conference Wednesday August 30th to proactively announce to the media that the plant would likely explode within the next several hours.

Why didn't he wait until the explosion happened? Why not just keep his mouth shut and hope for the best, and maybe the media wouldn't notice? After all, in the week after Harvey struck, other chemical plants and oil refineries across the area released millions of pounds of toxic and carcinogenic pollutants into the air and floodwaters, but they all stayed under the radar while attention zeroed in only on Arkema.[31]

For Arkema, the answer was easy. Hiding from the press is what "bad" companies do. It's not what trustworthy companies do.

Withholding information will provoke more media coverage, keeping negative information longer in play and raising the odds of reputational damage. Withholding information that later comes to light can not only cause additional media attention, but that media attention may be even greater than the attention initially generated when the crisis first breaks.

As part of my doctoral dissertation, I surveyed a representative sampling of journalists in the Washington, D.C. market. Ninety-five percent of journalists surveyed said they would be more suspicious of a company if they found that the company had withheld critical information, or tried to cover it up, than if the company had released the information proactively.

Nine out of ten said knowing that the company had deliberately withheld information would cause them to dig deeper and harder for additional incriminating information. And an overwhelming majority (98%) of journalists said the fact that the company had tried to withhold information would prompt additional coverage.

3.7.2 Cover-Ups Can Lead to Ugly Unveilings

In the Ford/Firestone crisis[32] as well as the Uber hacking crisis [see section 6.2.1], the crises had less to do with mistakes being made and much more to do with public disgust over cover-ups that lasted until someone else exposed them. Organizations typically fare better by owning up, apologizing, making reparations and taking corrective actions. All of which can be significantly less expensive than litigation and a ruined reputation.

3.7.2.1 Case Study – Flint water crisis (2016)

In January 2016, a federal emergency was declared in Flint, Michigan because of elevated lead levels in the city drinking water system. The Michigan Department of Environmental Quality came under fire for compromising the health of its residents (especially children) and blaming it on a lack of funding.[33]

Lesson learned: Cover-ups and finger-pointing lead to loss of trust.

3.7.2.2 Case Study – Volkswagen (2015)

In 2015, VW got caught red-handed using "defeat devices" and deceit in VWs from 2009-2015. The software allowed the vehicles to meet emissions standards in the lab, while on the roads, the vehicles emitted nitrogen oxide at up to 40 times federal standards. Buyers were particularly upset because the alleged "clean diesel" technology cost them a premium. VW stock took a 30% nosedive.[34]

In the months following the discovery that VW had cheated on emissions tests, the company struggled to maintain its cover-up, claiming first that its cars had a technical problem that was causing tailpipe emissions to soar on the road… later that it was just "the mistakes of a few people" (even though the scandal involved 11 million vehicles), and then skirted making restitution to European customers (though good-will payments were issued to US customers) because the practice was technically legal in Europe.[35]

It took more than a year before VW finally admitted guilt.[36]

And like Ford, which may have borne some portion of the blame in the Firestone crisis of 2000, respected supplier Bosch agreed to a $327.5 million settlement in 2017 for its part in the deception.[37]

Lesson learned: Don't exacerbate a cover-up. Stakeholders who are left feeling duped for paying a premium for emperor's clothes won't take kindly.

3.7.2.3 Case Study – Princess Cruise Lines (2016)

In 2016, Princess Cruise Lines was forced to pay a $40 million penalty for dumping waste into the ocean and then attempting to cover it up, including ordering subordinates to lie to authorities.[38]

Lesson learned: Cover-ups can lead to higher costs.

If all information is released when the crisis first breaks, journalists estimate their coverage of crisis stories could likely be over within the first 24-48 hours. However, when additional information comes to light – even as early as one day after the genesis of the crisis – the number of total stories increases. More damaging, though, is that the total number of stories is more spread out – increasing the length of time the story is kept "alive" and company reputation can continue to suffer damage. Also, subsequent attention is often more pronounced and more damaging than the initial spike of media attention. And since stock value typically remains low throughout the time period of most intense negative media coverage, allowing damaging information to seep out gradually can slow financial recovery.[39]

For decades, the Catholic church covered up for pedophile priests – sending them to retirement or rehabilitation rather than prosecuting them. It was a classic case of leaders listening to the justifications of advisors who told them it wasn't necessary to take such harsh steps, that they could back away short of the right – but hard – thing to do.

3.7.3 Being a Good Neighbor

Building trust means doing the right thing – even when the public may not find out.

It also means being an active force for good within the community – adding rather than just taking – whether it is required or not. Giving back, such as volunteering time and money to help where needed and not just paying taxes owed is what counts.

Arkema is France's largest chemical company, but in the United States, it is relatively unknown to most Americans. Arkema focused its community relations strategy on becoming known as a good neighbor within the communities where Arkema plants reside – building bridges, literally.

When the time came, Arkema wanted to be in the position of not having to say "trust us, we're a good company," when it would be so much more powerful and believable to have the community say it instead.

While most organizations focus their social media channels on marketing, I re-focused Arkema's social media channels to primarily highlight the company's community relations efforts. Take a look… and then compare what you find with the social media feeds of your favorite company.

Arkema on Facebook: https://www.facebook.com/ArkemaInc/

Arkema on Twitter: https://twitter.com/Arkema_Inc

Sure, you'll find some marketing boasts interspersed, but most posts are ultra-local in nature with no effort too small to mention – from local blood drives and Thanksgiving food roundups to care packages for the troops – whatever individual employees are passionate about and spend their time doing to help out the communities surrounding Arkema plants. Their message is clear: Arkema is an active, engaged member of the community too.

Like many companies aligned with science and engineering, Arkema finds value in focusing on its core competencies whenever possible when choosing programs to sponsor. The Science Teacher program is a popular community relations program sponsored by corporate headquarters for any plant that wants to hold a program locally in their community and it has been a large bridge to the communities. Many of the Arkema plants are situated in lower income locations where schools don't have a lot in the way of resources, so gifts of books and reading volunteer and mentoring programs have long been a way for Arkema employees to give within their communities.

Arkema's Science Teacher program includes identifying local elementary school teachers for a summertime program designed to team the teachers with Arkema scientists to together work through the materials and experiments found in commercially prepared science kits (which the teachers are at liberty to select and which are purchased by Arkema and donated to the schools). The extra mentoring allows the teachers to learn new science techniques and ways to make science interesting so they can teach their science classes with renewed enthusiasm come Fall. As with other science, technology, engineering and math (STEM) programs designed to reach 4th through 6th graders (the timeframe when children are most likely to lose interest in science-related careers), Arkema hopes the program will inspire students to stay engaged.

The program has been a hit with the schools surrounding Arkema plants where the program is held and teachers who have participated in the program become staunch advocates. They see a benefit in having Arkema as a neighbor – and that value far outweighs the downside of having a chemical plant next door, especially since – through the summertime interaction – they learn about safety procedures and steps the plant takes to minimize risk and share information.

3.7.4 Developing Unofficial Spokespersons Who Have Good Things to Say

Although the community relations program preceded my time at Arkema, I recognized the value it would have during a crisis and strongly promoted the strengthening of programs for each location as well as the use of Arkema's social media tools to publicize efforts. As mentioned earlier [see section 2.4.1], affected stakeholders are not particularly likely to consider official spokespersons the most trustworthy sources. But unofficial boosters who are known and trusted within the community and most importantly have nothing to gain from advocating on behalf of a company can be very influential.

I understood that if and when a crisis came, Arkema would be able to rely on these unofficial advocates to bolster what official spokespersons said and to act as counterpoints to negative comments. That's why we used social media to engage the community and to build on the long-term positive relationships developed over years of interaction. We knew that those who had something negative to say would turn to social media, and those who tuned in to what they had to say would be met with a story that didn't mesh with what the naysayers had to say.

3.7.4.1 Case Study – Unexpected Advocates During the Bristol Tote Spill (June 2014)

As mentioned earlier [see Section 2.5.4], a small chemical spill at Arkema's Bristol PA plant resulted in the principal of a local elementary school sheltering-in-place the school's children, even though a local "fun day" end-of-year carnival was taking place that day. It was of course a disappointment for the kids as well as the parent teacher organization which had spent the entire year fund-raising for the event.

Arkema reached out immediately afterwards to write a check for the full amount so the carnival could be rescheduled. Meanwhile, teachers who had participated in Arkema's Science Teacher Program through the years acted as unsolicited advocates amongst their peers. Rather than getting a bad rap for the accident and the inconvenience it caused, the school *thanked* Arkema for being a good neighbor.

Following is an unsolicited letter sent the day after Arkema's business unit president wrote a check to cover the carnival. It came from one of the teachers who had participated in Arkema's Science Teacher Program.

```
From: Heather Foster
Date:   06/11/2014 10:03 AM
Subject:        RE: Principal

        Seriously, no worries. We all know how great you guys are there.
Nancy and I said nothing but wonderful things about you guys yesterday.
We told them how you guys were awesome to us and that if you could
make this right, you would.

While some were disappointed, we all dealt with it. It comes with the
territory. You can say, we are used to it. No one is bad mouthing...
especially NOW... no harm...

Have a great one.
Take care! You guys are the best!

                        Heather Foster
                        Fourth Grade Teacher
                        Mary Devine Elementary School
```

Lesson learned: Doing the right thing can lead to unexpected advocates.

Questions for Further Thought and Discussion

> ➤ *In the Arkema press conferences, the same two questions kept
>   coming up. If you were in a similar situation as spokesperson and
>   the same question was raised a second time, what steps would you
>   take to ensure sufficient clarification?*
> ➤ *What steps can you take at your organization to make sure the
>   media can easily find good news about the organization during
>   times of crisis?*
> ➤ *Who are the unofficial spokespersons who would have something
>   positive to say about your organization if you were in a crisis,
>   and how can you cultivate them?*

➤ *What do you think about Arkema's decision to speak up and notify the media in advance of its crisis? Would you have done the same? Why or why not?*

Summary

Who trusts a chemical company? At Arkema, their neighbors do, as a result of the crisis strategies I put in place when I managed their crisis program in the years leading up to the crisis at Crosby TX in the wake of Hurricane Harvey. This chapter provided linchpin strategies for leading stakeholders to good news, creating advocates through community relations, and being the first to break your own bad news.

CHAPTER 4

NO SUCCESSFUL CRISIS RESPONSE

BEGINS ON THE DAY OF THE CRISIS

No successful crisis response begins on the day of the crisis. It takes preparation, not only to identify the likely risks but also to examine the organization's processes, culture and so forth to identify the less likely risks. Finding the potential crises that you don't see coming is an art. That's because the crisis management practitioner has to be able to look at business areas that she may know nothing about in a technical sense, and predict what could go wrong, even if it seems unlikely. Tiny things can mushroom quickly into very large problems.

As an example, Company A makes a fairly ordinary part that can be used in widgets in a lot of different markets. This is a reliable product line with a reliable supply line. It's profitable. There's not a lot to worry about. Each of the things that goes into making the part is pretty easy to get. But for one of those things, there is only one supplier. What happens if that supplier's production is shut down? That could be very damaging to Company A's reputation and business, especially if it is a critical supplier for Company X and Company Y, which will consider Company A to be unreliable if they fail to deliver.

The risk of supply chain failure may be among the foreseeable risks Company A has planned for as part of its business continuity and risk management planning, but too many companies become complacent thinking they've done their due diligence if they identify and plan for their most likely risks. They don't delve deeply enough into examining brand and reputation impacts that seem less likely but can be higher impact and they lack signal detectors to key them in to misaligned stakeholder perspectives or issues that are becoming problematic.

That's why it is so critical to plan for crises and to have, proactively, the elements in place to suss out potential crises the organization doesn't see coming and derail them before they happen. It takes a structure and process not only for responding to a disruption and resuming operations quickly, but to stand a better chance of *avoiding* crises entirely.

Ad hoc response built on the belief that we have good people who know how to run this company or organization is not as effective as planning and practicing for success. I'm not great with the sports analogies, but what sports team would consider *not* practicing their best strategy for winning a championship? Just because they've got top players, doesn't mean those people will be adept at interacting with each other under pressure and with speed. The team has to work together to figure out where their vulnerabilities are, how to play off their strengths, what resources are needed. They may watch hours of game film to analyze where they can perform better. They review every step of how they anticipate performing the job they've done countless times before, just to make it a little bit better, smoother, faster.

This chapter covers:

- *Building your crisis team and concept of operations.*
- *Tailoring a solution that works for your unique circumstances.*
- *Streamlining your approval process.*
- *Strategic drills to armchair-quarterback (in advance) where you might be jumping the tracks.*

4.1 Building a Team and Concept of Operations

The US public sector uses an incident command system (ICS) or a unified command structure for operating efficiently. It is considered a best practice. In fact, it has been so widely touted by former military and government users, that many corporate entities have structured their crisis teams to match the categories of Administrative, Operations, Planning, and Logistics silos. Government and the military already have most of those entities, so that structure makes sense. Unfortunately, for many corporate entities, it's a shoe that may not fit and no amount of squeezing is going to make the fit work well. Government and business are inherently different. [More on the limitations of relying on "best practices" in the next chapter.]

The concept is based on the goal of finding a universal operating structure that can be used by all agencies and public entities so that they can effectively and seamlessly work together in a plug-and-play fashion. The fire department in one jurisdiction operates essentially the same way as the next county over so that when they need to rely on mutual aid agreements and share resources in big events, they know how the other team is going to operate. Everyone knows who is in charge and the person in charge can assign roles that are uniform and understood by all participants.

It works for the public sector when responding to emergencies because that's how they're structured in their command and control environment, but the premise can be awkward when it comes to corporations because that's just not how corporations are organized. Most corporations don't necessarily (although some do) fit neatly into the identified ICS buckets.

Even two companies that do substantially the same things often approach their business in vastly different ways with vastly different philosophies. (Think of how often you hear of mergers gone bad when the projected economies of scale don't pan out.)

Perhaps Finance can work with the parameters of the Administrative branch. Maybe Engineering might fit under Operations... (though maybe Planning or Logistics would work better? It's not really clear and heavily dependent on the individual organization). Communications can align with the Public Information Officer role... But where does HR fit? Legal? And who is going to tell execs that their effective span of control can be no more than seven people?[40]

After many years of touting ICS as an appropriate best practice model for structuring a corporate emergency response team, the international standard on business continuity and emergency management, NFPA 1600, now acknowledges that although an organization's incident management system should clearly define how the organization will coordinate with on-scene public sector responders as they arrive and take over emergency response, whatever structure that best fits the organization is appropriate.[41]

There are many potential models available and no one model that best fits all organizations.

4.1.1 Tailor a Solution That Works for Your Unique Circumstances

Your organization should look at the guidance available and tailor a solution that best fits your organization's management style and structure, culture, operating system.

There will, of course, be a certain amount of command and control. Someone has to run the show, so you will need a crisis management team that consists of people who have the authority to make decisions within a clear structure and with a well-established process.

It would be a mistake to assume that you can wing crisis management in the same way you would never just assume a bunch of talented players could handle a game without any structure or practice. I have found repeatedly that without structure and a clear process that gets regularly exercised and improved, someone who believes they need to be involved (and should be) gets left out.

Identify what roles should be part of the response and management. Ascertain whether there will need to be an emergency or incident team focused on initial threats and response to life, health, or safety concerns at the facility level. Are there support functions like HR, Communications, Security that advise leadership on key concerns and support with tactics?

Do team members have the authority to make strategy decisions on behalf of the organization or are these team members the "doers" who make things happen but then must leave the most strategic decision and direction making to the C-suite? If the latter, there should be clear-cut thresholds for what decisions and actions can be taken by what level of the crisis structure, when they activate, how they convene, and what authorities they have.

Develop a concept of operations of how the team will perform. What are the triggers for convening? Where will they operate? Is a dedicated physical space even necessary? Many teams get bogged down identifying where to place the war room and how to equip it.

Best practice provides a great deal of guidance on this, and, in today's environment, most of it is absolutely unnecessary. You probably really don't need an operating theater or crisis "war room" set aside just for this purpose—any conference room (physical or virtual) will do. You don't need special supplies, files, or physical manuals if you have access to laptops, smart phones and collaboration tools. I am aware of many companies that do have a crisis room at the ready. Unless it is easily occupied by another function the other 99 percent of the time when it is not needed for crisis purposes, its upkeep is likely to be unjustifiable.

4.1.2 Do You Really Need a Crisis War Room?

There are plenty of manuals identifying what your organization's crisis meeting room should contain. Jane's Crisis Communications Handbook (which also has plenty of *good* information) lists the following recommendations for the well-stocked crisis center[42]:

- Phones
- Contact list printouts (internal, media, other key stakeholders)

- Computers with web access and email capability
- Printers & fax machines
- Back-up generators, batteries, food, water and medical kits
- Speakerphone for conference calls
- Whiteboards
- Televisions w/cable/satellite hook-up
- Ability to record broadcasts
- Two-way radios, other means of monitoring the situation
- Office supplies – pens, paper, mirror
- Internal policy documents…

This may have been a fine list 15 or 20 years ago, but unless your company is part of the critical infrastructure (such as a utility company handing the fallout from a weather disaster) or unless you are a public sector agency co-located in an Emergency Operations Center (EOC) to coordinate multi-jurisdictional response, the laptops and smart phones of your team members are likely to provide most of what you need. Face-to-face interaction in a physical location is not always necessary.

Review the explanations below detailing why each of these items was considered crucial for the standard war room, then make your own judgment call how your well-stocked crisis center should morph in order to keep up with today's environment, or even whether there is a benefit to setting aside a room for this purpose.

Phones – for dialing out. In some cases, phones were also expected to be supplied in the press center so that journalists covering the story would have a means of filing their articles and also in the event cell capacity is limited in an emergency. Today, you can assume most individuals will have their own smart phones. Although cell capacity during emergencies has increased dramatically in recent years in most regions, it would be wise to test whether wireless connectivity is an issue locally and ensure there are adequate electrical outlets (for charging phones and laptops).

Contact list printouts (internal, media, other key stakeholders) – will electronic storage and smart lists help you keep them fresher today?

Computers with web access and email capability – in case people forgot to bring their laptops, the war room was expected to have ample desktops. Survey your organizational environment. How many people have been issued a desktop instead of a laptop for their day-to-day work? Do people take their laptops home on a regular basis or do they leave them at their desks overnight? Gauge whether maintaining desktops is necessary. Most organizations find they unnecessarily take up space.

Printers and fax machines – access to printers may still be useful (especially if people have forgotten their laptops). But is it necessary to have a dedicated printer in the war room? In the 1990s, fax machines were sometimes used to file news stories. Do you need them at all now?

Back-up generators, batteries, food, water and medical kits – if you are going to assign a physical space where people are expected to congregate to manage the crisis over an extended period of time, these items may be needed. For many organizations, if the building's power is out, you may find the crisis team members will likely tolerate generator power for only as long as the bathrooms are still operational.

Speakerphone for conference calls – could be useful, assuming the team needs to co-locate to meet, rather than dialing in to a conference number from individual cell phones. Still, most smartphones will handle speaker mode and conference calls with little effort.

Whiteboards – to display updated information and a chronology of the situation so the entire team can stay abreast.

Televisions with cable or satellite hook-up and the ability to record broadcasts – in the days before broadcasts were accessible on the Internet, this allowed the crisis team to remain connected to the outside world and to stay abreast of what the media were reporting. The need has been supplanted as long as you have team members keeping tabs virtually.

Two-way radios, other means of monitoring the situation – perhaps. Does your organization have access to cell phones, email? There are emergency notification apps which can be appropriate for most organizations.

Office supplies – pens, paper, mirror – again, paper and pens were for those who forgot their laptops. The mirror was meant to be used to check whether there was broccoli in one's teeth before stepping out to address the media as spokesperson.

Internal policy documents – especially if they are not electronically available. This will necessitate a storage cabinet and regular updates to keep them current. Is it worth the space and manpower for your organization?

4.1.3 Alternates Can't Be a Lesser Caste

Finally, do you have adequate alternate crisis team members? Are they drilled with the same frequency as primaries? Do they have the same authorities to act in the absence of the primaries? In some cases, in some organizations, there are no obvious alternates. Shoehorning an alternate in place just to have an alternate is a bad idea.

In one organization I worked with, I came across an alternate to the HR primary team member who had zero experience in HR but was a good "people person" (his words) so he was the identified alternate. But in the event of crisis, he'd have had no idea what policies were in place, what contractors were available to provide employee assistance programs (EAP) nor how to activate them, he had no access to people's emergency contact information, he'd never been trained in death notifications, etc. I quickly replaced him with another HR person in another section of the region who was a much better match for the HR alternate role, even though that person was not on site. In this instance, being on site was no match for being able to actually fulfill the alternate role, albeit remotely.

Through drilling, a similar issue came up with regard to finding alternates for the presidents of the business units. What if the primary decision-maker were out of cell service range for many hours – or severely injured or killed? Shouldn't there be an alternate who can make decisions on behalf of the business line? It became a real sticking point because despite the push to name an alternate, the honest answer was that the decisions really couldn't be delegated down. Over and over during the drill, any decision that was made by an alternate was simply overridden when the business unit president was finally consulted. Delegating down just wasn't going to work. In this case, the only choice was to delegate *up* to the company's CEO.

This strategy might be worth considering. Alternates don't have to be second-class citizens who aren't really empowered to make decisions. Consider delegating up instead if a decision absolutely can't wait until the primary decision-maker is reachable again.

4.1.4 Practice What You Preach

Once identified and structured, *use* the team you have identified and structured. Practice the team so they can operate successfully together (more on that in a moment). More important, though, is convening the whole team and using the actual process devised – or change the team and process if actual incidents bear out a different reality! There is no sense or benefit of having a process on paper that bears no resemblance to reality or it will be an unusable, unsuitable ill-fitting crisis process that will fail when most needed.

Use low-grade incidents and realistic scenario drills as practice sessions for the real thing. If the process isn't followed in low-level incidents, dissect and analyze why the process didn't work as well as intended. Be prepared for the possibility that the process or team structure was idealistic instead of rational. Have you built your process on a "best practice" model that worked in another organization but doesn't really fit the way your current organization operates? If so, it may not be best practice for your organization and to force a structure and concept of operations that doesn't fit can lead to resentment, finger-pointing, and feelings that the team will never get it right, rather than pride and confidence.

Even once you've got a workable concept of operations, it may still take several failures before the team gets the hang of it and agrees – together – to a suit that fits best. It can't be forced.

For example, in one organization I worked with, the process (on paper) was to bring the entire crisis management team together for the initial crisis assessment meeting then release non-necessary crisis team members if they did not believe they had anything to contribute to the situation at hand.

It seemed a good process on paper but wasn't always implemented in reality. Especially the day the organization faced a kidnapping crisis. Because of the sensitivity of the event, leadership wanted the situation to be kept close to the vest and did not want information to leak out, for good reasons (it could compromise the safety of the person who was being held) as well as bad (the organization did not want employees to panic and fear for their own safety). So a decision was made to bring only the "core" (their words) crisis team together and exclude all the less-necessary roles that were not pertinent to the decision-making that needed to happen.

On the face of it, IT did not appear to be a necessary team member. Cut and dried. Quick elimination.

The next day it became apparent that the kidnapped person's phone had been compromised – names, contact details, addresses – putting more people at risk of being targeted. Had the IT crisis team member been brought into the team deliberations from the start, they likely would have not only pointed out the risk and vulnerability of this occurring, but also the solution of shutting the phone down remotely.

Most team members think in silos – focused on their areas of expertise and what they can contribute. Unless each team member is brought to the table, there are pieces of the response that can easily be overlooked until it is much too late to do be truly effective and it becomes a scramble.

In this case, it was a learning opportunity and an "aha!" growth and solidification moment.

Many months later, one of the company's databases was hacked. IT, which had been burned in the earlier event, took the lead ensuring that the full crisis team was convened for a briefing on what had happened and to make decisions on next steps. Again, it seemed pretty cut-and-dried.

An administrative account had been compromised and hackers were able to access a site where potential customers registered to get more information on and pricing for the organization's products. IT dismissed the hack as relatively inconsequential because the site was not used for product sales and therefore no credit cards or financial information had been exposed. They recommended that since the situation was under control and the administrative account had been shut down, those who had registered need not be informed of the event.

I asked for more information about what IT meant when they said customers had registered. Were registrants asked to create usernames and passwords and did the hackers have access to those passwords? The answer was yes.

My recommendation to the chief technology officer was that the theft of user names and passwords could have been the real intent because people often use the same credentials for different sites. Therefore, every one of the registrants should be told about the hack and urged to immediately change the passwords for any other accounts where they'd used the same credentials.

The "win" in the second event was that it re-confirmed the benefit of pulling the entire team together—even for cases when it seemed cut-and-dried that some team members were not necessary. The team decided that the individual team members, as experts in their own areas, would be the ones to determine whether to excuse themselves since a non-expert doesn't necessarily know what they don't know. Once excused, released team members should remain up to speed on briefings (through notes shared between team meetings) and should be prepared to jump back into play at a moment's notice if the circumstances change.

4.1.5 Don't Let the Train Derail Because the Track Doesn't Fit

Although most companies in the public sphere face a multitude of potential crises, no two crises are identical. For that reason, I'm not a big fan of scripting out exact plans for how a crisis should be handled. There are too many things that could happen differently, throwing the cascade of what is supposed to happen – and by whom – off if one domino is out of place. Having a flexible capability in place to act – no matter what the emergency is – is critical.

Emergency calling trees have fallen out of favor as a means of notifying and providing instructions to employees in an emergency because if just one person doesn't get and pass on the message, the whole system could fail. Similarly, step-by-step crisis plans itemizing exactly what is supposed to happen for every conceivable scenario can derail if one link in the chain is broken and doesn't go according to plan.

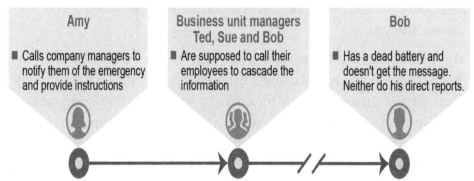

Fig. 4-1. One broken link can derail the plan.

4.2 Approvals

Across industries, I've noticed that the single most important thing that drills bring out is just how long it takes to do certain things in real time. This is especially true when trying to jump on something early before all the facts are in.

Another thing that I've noticed is that the larger the team of decision-makers, the slower decisions get made. So, instead of leaving the wording to communications professionals (with approval by appropriate experts for accuracy), the team gets bogged down in wordsmithing. This is a problem when you need to acknowledge an issue and insofar as it is possible, shape the narrative.

At one company, to speed things up when it was clear that this was happening, I put into place a two-person core rapid-communications team (enhanced with a third person if we needed an expert to ensure that what we were saying was factual).

The rapid response communications core team consisted of me and the sharpest, hardest-to-get-along-with lawyer on the legal team (because legal always wants to be involved in what is being said).

I sought empowerment from senior leadership for rapid-response communications so that, as long as the two of us could agree on wording, the two of us had the authority to release the communication.

Subsequent communications and decision-making would get into additional vetting with additional team members, but this strategy allowed us to get our initial communications out quickly.

4.3 Strategic Drilling (With a Mirror) Can Avoid Lawsuits

This is not a primer on how to create and execute a drill. It is an explanation for why it is necessary to practice crisis response and how to use drills more strategically by allowing your team members to discover improvements rather than just check a required box.

To use a sports analogy again, players need to develop the muscle memory and, in general, players who know where they're supposed to be and what they're supposed to do – and when – will be more successful. There's a saying in the military that no plan survives first contact with the enemy. That is why soldiers train and train – when a plan falls apart, they can rely on their training to guide them.

I've seen plenty of employees drag their feet during fire drills or go to great lengths to hide out to avoid them. Or who consider themselves too important to participate.

In some organizations I've worked with, we've sometimes held announced drills, even going so far as to put the date and time on everyone's calendar so they could schedule important meetings around the event and not complain about the interruption. In essence, that takes away the excuse of not participating. But it was always a tradeoff. If we found that people were abusing the knowledge of when the drill was, we'd go back to having to surprise them with an unannounced drill that very well could be interrupting meetings that took weeks to set up. In my book, getting more people to walk the walk and to practice rather than hide is a win.

A lot of it has to do with respect. And leadership. When volunteer floor wardens are empowered and respected, other employees will follow their instructions. I've witnessed a floor warden (who was an administrative assistant) bark at a business unit president to tell him to hustle during a shelter-in-place drill. Those floor wardens got all occupants of the building to the designated shelter-in-place location in 15 seconds. As with so many things, this starts at the top. Without sincere leadership buy-in, this would not have been possible.

4.3.1 Case Study – Rick Rescorla's Drills Saved Lives

On September 11, 2001, Rick Rescorla led Morgan Stanley's 2687 employees out of the World Trade Center. After watching how long it took to evacuate following the 1993 attack, he frequently and relentlessly drilled employees with surprise fire drills to ensure they knew exactly what to do (quickly and calmly) if a terrorist strike ever occurred again, something that he was so certain would happen again, he had urged Morgan Stanley to relocate from the World Trade Centers to New Jersey. Rescorla – a decorated Vietnam vet – trained his company to drop everything, no matter how important, to practice evacuations.

Rescorla and a handful of his security team members were last seen heading back up the stairs of the World Trade Center September 11th to make sure all their people were out. All but Rescorla and his team were out – because of Rick Rescorla's relentless drills.[43]

Lesson learned: leadership buy-in and taking drills seriously can make a very big difference.

But strategic crisis drills go beyond mass training. The more realistic the scenario is as well as the seriousness with which participants take the drill, the better crisis team members will respond and work together in an actual situation. Challenging team members to apply a framework to an unexpected situation – rather than expecting them to walk through scripted actions to pass a pass/fail test – can provide interest and improvements.

4.3.2 Drilling to Let the Team Discover Solutions

Drills can be an important tool to make the case for solutions. Using a drill scenario built to put the impact of a prospective or problematic policy into a realistic context can help demonstrate the policy's effectiveness or show its inherent flaws. It provides the opportunity to consider whether Plan B is actually better than Plan A.

Drills can also provide leadership with an opportunity to do a realistic walkthrough of how a contemplated decision might play out from other perspectives. This allows them to get some insight into how stakeholders may see the situation.

Finding the flaws in assumptions about how a business is run, and how dangerous its assumptions might turn out to be in a crisis, is as much an art as it is a skill. It takes a keen ability to extend the implications of business decisions into the most probable (but also potential) outcomes. A drill can provide the opportunity for executives to see first-hand other potential outcomes and how a situation might play out differently from how they assume it will.

In one of the organizations I worked with, social media monitoring picked up a comment linking the company to a medical device permanently implanted in the body that was causing painful problems at a high rate. The company itself did not make such devices, only a part of them. Users were gearing up for a class action lawsuit and had involved activist Erin Brockovich.

Because the company's literature specified that no medical grade materials that the company made should be implanted in the body for longer than 30 days, this group contemplating the lawsuit had begun speculating that perhaps it was the company's part of the product that was causing their bodies to reject the device. The logic was understandable, if completely flawed.

When the company I was working with explored what its product was actually being used for, we discovered that the device maker had listed in its government filings everything that went into the device. Everything. But the part that we produced was only part of the means for inserting the device – meaning that, at most, it might have been in contact with the body for moments.

The company was able to straighten that out relatively quickly, and when the lawsuit was eventually filed against the manufacturer, our company was not dragged in.

To be fair, we had no reason to believe our product was harmful, we had just never researched use in the human body for longer than one month – and besides, we had also already made clear to our key distributers that the material had not been tested for use longer than 30 days, so technically, we had no responsibility for what downstream producers were doing with it. I say technically because it often doesn't matter what your legal risk is – when your company name gets dragged through the mud, it's difficult to get the mud off.

We had no idea who the distributors were selling the product to. We had no idea what those customers were using the product for, nor whether they'd been informed that it had not been tested for use longer than 30 days and shouldn't be used in permanent devices – which at least in this case, it was not.

The light bulb moment for me was that our company was completely surprised at how its medical grade product could have been used – and we had no idea that company material was being used in or with this device.

But what if there were other manufacturers using our material for implantables? What if next time we discovered our material wasn't just in a catheter that was removed within minutes but instead had truly been left in the body against our instructions? Could we just wash our hands of liability because this information had been passed on to the distributor we sold the material to? Or would our stakeholders consider us responsible for ensuring the information got passed on to the end user in case the distributor didn't? Would it actually matter if the courts found us to be not liable – when fighting the battle in court (or settling) would undoubtedly be very expensive regardless?

So, instead of breathing a sigh of relief that we had caught this one in time and moved our company out of the spotlight, I used the situation to create a realistic scenario to explore those "what ifs."

Up until drilling with this scenario, the company had been taking the stance that it was okay to wash our hands because we'd done our part by informing the distributors and our responsibility ended there.

As a result of looking at these issues and playing out the potential consequences through this other lens, company leadership decided to put in place a more comprehensive solution to ensure end-use customers (not just distributors) were also made aware our medical grade products were not intended for long term use, almost certainly heading off future litigation.

4.4 Do the Right Thing

When it comes to perception risks which could affect reputation, it is often better to err on the side of doing the right thing, especially when the impact of what you hope doesn't happen is going to be significant in the event it does happen after all. When it comes down to it, the public expects companies that it believes to be "good" companies to do the right thing and can be sorely disappointed when they find out they lied, cheated, covered up just like a "bad" company would have. In fact, good companies are held to a higher standard than bad companies.[44]

4.4.1 Case Study – Fans Expected More from Apple

An organization with a "good" reputation may find it is held to a higher standard and its proponents are more disappointed and let down when they go off-mark.

In January 2018, two of Apple's largest shareholders began putting pressure on the company to try to influence the way Apple markets to children. The stockholders cited recent studies linking cellphone overuse with feelings of addiction, anxiety, and depression, particularly among teens. Apple's shareholders have begun pushing for more protections for kids and more choices for parents to decide how much of an app's content is accessible to their kids and other tools to help them limit their kids' screen time.[45]

This signals a shift in the way the public is viewing what it believes is okay for tech companies to wash their hands of and where their responsibility for a problem begins and ends.

Lesson learned: For many years tech giant Apple was a trusted friend, until its consumers were left feeling cheated. Being let down by a trusted friend is more disappointing than being disappointed by a company you never really trusted to do the right thing in the first place.

4.4.2 Case Study – University of Maryland Medical Center Patient Dumping (2018)

In January 2018, the University of Maryland Medical Center discharged an impaired woman to a bus stop out front of the hospital, wearing only a hospital gown and nothing else – in freezing temperatures. The woman could barely walk and did not appear to be able to speak. The "patient dumping" episode was caught on video by bystander Imamu Baraka and triggered an uproar of indignation because people expect more from a well-respected hospital charged with care.[46]

Fig. 4-2. Imamu Baraka's patient dumping video can be found at
https://www.washingtonpost.com/news/local/wp/2018/01/10/video-shows-apparently-
incapacitated-half-naked-woman-put-out-in-cold-by-baltimore-
hospital/?utm_term=.4ec826abcc92

Lesson learned: people expect more from "good" organizations and hold them to a higher standard.

4.4.3 Case Study – Amtrak Derailments Disappoint (2017 and 2015)

Public calls for reform after a train collision in 2008 that killed 25 people led to a Congressional mandate that major railroads needed to install positive train control safety systems by the end of 2015.

Then, even after Amtrak 188 derailed near Philadelphia in 2015 (killing eight) after taking a curve much too fast, the mandate on safety system installation was pushed back three more years because railroads complained the cost was too high and threatened boycotts. Although Amtrak promised to reform, the safety system still wasn't in use before Amtrak Cascades 501's derailment in Washington State in 2017, because Amtrak balked at spending money on safety unless it absolutely had to.[47]

Complying with the letter of the law while simultaneously showing what appears to be callous indifference by refusing to go beyond what is absolutely required, especially if victims are left bearing the cost, is a surefire reputation crusher. It's not the mark of what stakeholders expect from "good" companies.

Lesson learned: just skating by can be a reputation crusher. Consumers expect more from the organizations they trust.

Summary

No successful crisis response begins on the day of the crisis. Successful crisis responses are planned and manifested in advance. This chapter explained how to build your organization's crisis team and concept of operations with solutions that are tailored specifically for your organization's unique circumstances, then challenged with strategic drills.

Questions for Further Thought and Discussion

> *Do you have a crisis war room at your organization? Why or why not? (If not, how do you plan to convene crisis team members?)*
> *What concept of operations and incident management system do you use to govern how your crisis management team will operate?*
> *Have you pre-approved statements for use during crisis?*
> *What is a policy your organization could benefit from scripting an exercise scenario around?*

CHAPTER 5

WHAT ARE THE CARDINAL RULES OF BUSINESS CONTINUITY AND WHO SET THEM?

There is a great deal of literature on best practices in public relations, even though the "best practices" may have little or no research to back them. Beyond case studies and anecdotes (with each repetition giving further credence to what amount to little more than assumptions), very few crisis communications principles have been tested. Practitioners have simply accepted these theories without empirical data.[48]

Another problem with "best practices" is that they may be set in a particular moment. Speaking broadly, best practices established many years ago would hardly be adequate for most crises today, yet many people stick with best practices blindly because they are, after all, best practices. Instead, it's imperative to challenge the cardinal rules. That means putting aside cookie-cutter solutions in order to create tailored solutions that more soundly bolster an organization's capability to mitigate and recover from a crisis or disruption.

This chapter covers:

- *Challenging the cardinal rules of business continuity to determine whether they're truly best practice for your organization.*
    - o *Disaster recovery facility in another region?*
    - o *Templates?*
    - o *Consultants?*
    - o *Hotsites?*
    - o *Risk analysis?*
    - o *Crisis room?*
    - o *Nurture media contacts?*

5.1 Rule 1: Put Your Disaster Recovery Facility in Another Area of the Country?

The purpose of a business continuity plan (BCP) is simple: to protect the viability of the company – to resume business operations as soon as possible after a business disruption. It sets forth the steps the organization must take within the first hours and days to continue to operate despite the disruption to normal operations.

Best practice in planning for business continuity often includes ensuring there is a disaster recovery facility in another region of the country. This was considered a best practice in the 1990s, when many companies believed their biggest likelihood of disruption would be a natural disaster affecting the company's main servers. Today, instituting an alternate facility in another region is still considered best practice by neophytes who overlook the need to focus and bolster business continuity plans against the even more real possibility that a disruption may come from, for example, cybercrime rather than natural disaster.

5.2 Rule 2: Use a Template?

When I took over the business continuity planning for one large company, I discovered that previous planning had been done through templates and delegation. Each location was expected to identify a person who would be responsible for developing the business continuity plan by filling in the blanks and following the instructions in the template. No one wanted this job, so it was typically delegated to an administrative assistant. Without clear understanding of what was really being asked for or needed or why it was needed, the delegated individual would do the best they could to fill in the blanks to complete their plan.

In this case, the template indicated the need to put in place manual workarounds for every technology process, and toward that end, each office was to gather a disaster kit of templates, tools and documentation in order to accomplish these manual workarounds. These kits were carted off to off-site storage outside the area and stored at great expense. There they remained for years. Curious, I recalled the kits to see what was inside, and discovered the kits included reams of paper and boxes of pens and pencils. Obviously, the planners thought that if they weren't able to use computers, they'd simply take notes the old-fashioned way.

5.3 Rule 3: Business Continuity Plans Should Be Written by a Professional?

Although filling in the blanks of a template with no context may lead to less desirable plans, so too can putting the planning only in the hands of certified business continuity planners. Without the input of subject matter experts *and* plan users, the plans can become idealistic, impractical, and overly complicated. It takes a marriage of business continuity plan-trained coaching staff empowered to elicit the right answers from subject matter experts (not administrative assistants for those subject matter experts) to develop usable plans.

Similarly, I always insist on reviewing and challenging the plans myself and then sitting down with the highest ranking person within that business unit (along with the subject matter experts, so they'll get good facetime with their boss or boss' boss and due credit – very important in empowering workable solutions) to explain what is in the plans, taking and incorporating their feedback, and then getting their sign-off.

Although I am a member of the NFPA 1600 Technical Committee, which continually updates the national standard on, and best practices for, emergency management, business continuity and crisis management, I don't just follow the standard as a template. Instead, I ensure every plan for every organization I work with gets tailored to fit the individual needs and risks of the organization.

5.4 Rule 4: Contract a Hotsite?

Are disaster recovery hot sites (or commercial disaster recovery locations where an enterprise's data processing operations can be moved in the event the enterprise's data center is rendered inoperable and which allows the business to continue or quickly resume network operations) absolutely necessary? In some cases yes, but often the answer is that the organization may be able to make do with far less than they've been led to believe by rote following of best practice.

In one organization I worked with, the company insisted on maintaining a costly contract because that was considered "best practice." Never mind that when the headquarters location moved some years later, the alternate facility was no longer in a separate region, it was three miles away. They had iris scanners for our key staff and leadership and that was high tech and cool.

But we weren't able to identify in advance who would need the facility, and scope creep had set in with an increasing number of requests for seats.

I challenged the large number of seats set aside for payroll and finance personnel. Certainly, what they did was critical to the organization. But when I asked why so many seats were afforded to these particular departments, I was told that it was because other departments were better positioned to continue operating if the office building were inaccessible because they had taken steps to work from home and be self-reliant, but that, whereas other departments abided by regular office hours, payroll and finance were often in the office early and worked until late. It had become a cultural conviction in these two departments that team members did not need to take their laptops home overnight because once home, they had no intention of doing additional work.

Delving deeper, I discovered that team members in other departments were no less critical and no less dedicated. In fact, they often took laptops home and continued working remotely so the number of hours put in each day was similar. Yet these other departments were in a far more resilient position because, if something were to happen to the office location, they'd be able to continue work from their remote location and they had tested out the concept until it was just as fluid as working at the office; whereas the payroll and finance departments would have had no other option than to wait a minimum of 24 hours for the alternate site to be prepared for their use, then get themselves to the alternate site (through perhaps hazardous outside conditions) and then take up a majority of the seats. And the company was paying hundreds of thousands of dollars to retain all this unnecessary space at the alternate site.

Once reconfigured with more realistic parameters in place (including a stricter requirement that the majority of critical personnel from *every* department needed to take their laptops home as a business continuity measure), and a stipulation that each department would receive a roughly equal number of seats that they could allocate amongst themselves, whether for those who had not taken laptops home or for department heads and their key staff to have a physical location where they could meet face-to-face to make decisions, (they kept insisting this was necessary though it never bore out in real life), we had the opportunity to get a pretty good idea of just how much space we would likely need in a disaster situation.

Sometime later, power across the region went down as the result of a storm and left the office without electricity for several days so we were forced to activate our contract with the alternate site. I had multiple calls from concerned managers asking just how strictly they'd be held to their allocated number of seats. Inevitably, there were employees who were hit by the power outages in their own homes, had no power backup, and needed the alternate-site seats because their homes were in dead zones.

109

But the majority of the seats went unoccupied because – unsurprisingly – no one (critical or not) who could work remotely wanted to face the roads to get to the alternate site. Managers didn't want to come in to meet face-to-face when they could phone in. Payroll and finance staff had their laptops at home.

It certainly did allow us to make the case for cross-training individuals in other locations to be able to take over certain critical functions from unimpacted locations elsewhere in the event of a weather emergency in which our critical people couldn't work remotely because they'd left their laptops at work, didn't have power or connectivity at home, or driving conditions to get to the alternate site were too hazardous.

But that assumes the business disruption is the result of a weather event. Getting to the alternate site wouldn't have made a whit of difference in a cyberattack.

I am not doing work for that company any longer, but I would be surprised if the IT department is still able to make the argument that the company needs as many seats today.

5.5 Rule 5: Build Around a Risk Analysis?

You may want to start with a risk analysis which identifies the risks your organization is likely to face and prioritizes them based on likelihood of happening and the consequence if that risk does occur, but it is not always necessary to put a lot of expense into this.

NFPA 1600 has a good list of hazards you can use as a starting point.[49] Assess which hazards are likely for your organization. I don't want to oversimplify this, because an analysis can get quite detailed, quantified, and expensive. People make careers out of risk assessments. But in the end, no matter how specific and how much quantification goes into the analysis, it is still going to be no more than a best guess as to what the most likely set of risks for your organization will be. And organizations that mitigate only for the most likely risks may leave themselves wide open to other risks. A 100-year flood or earthquake risk may seem like something that we can put off mitigating until next year because complacency allows us to convince ourselves the likelihood of happening is outside our lifetime (and besides the budget is tight).

A better approach is to mitigate for high *impact* risks, regardless of likelihood or likely frequency.

For example, one of the companies I worked for had become complacent when it came to some of its supply chain risks. In one case, there was a raw material critical to one business unit's production, but a glitch in the supply chain seemed extremely low risk since 100 percent of the raw material was bought from the company right next door. How could there possibly be a failure in the supply chain? Why bother mitigating a one-in-a-million risk by purchasing some percentage of the supply from elsewhere?

I was able to make the case for looking at risk through the lens of impact rather than likelihood the day that a freak storm sent a lightning bolt into the raw material next door, obliterating our entire supply of critical raw material and sending the company scrambling to find a new source.

5.5.1 Case Study – Sprint Loses 911 Functionality (2016)

Risk assessments which identify what the most likely and highest priority risks are so that the organization can mitigate against them, can leave an organization complacent that they've got their risks "covered." Although that's not a bad approach, risk managers often convince themselves it isn't worth preparing for "unlikely" disruptions. Rather than looking at a situation vis-a-vis its likelihood, it would be better, instead, to plan for high impact events, no matter how unlikely they seem. Besides, mitigating high priority risks with contingency plans still doesn't mean the mitigation will be foolproof.

For example, a series of failures in backup systems in 2016, left customers of the Sprint network without the ability to contact 911 to report life-threatening emergencies for 12 hours.

First there was a transformer fire that caused an electrical outage in the DC, Maryland and Virginia region. Generators were the go-to backup but they ran out of fuel after a short while because of a stuck or broken valve. The battery-powered backup to the backup ran out of juice as well.

According to best practice, Sprint had done everything right. They'd not only mitigated the risk with a backup, but also had a backup to that backup, therefore decreasing the likelihood an incident would happen in the first place. Instead of focusing on what would be done if Sprint lost its ability to place critical calls, regardless of the reason, it had instead conditioned itself to believe it was fully prepared.[50]

Lesson learned: risk assessments aren't foolproof, they're just someone's best guess. Focus more on impact than likelihood.

5.6 Rule 6: Set Aside a Crisis War Room?

Challenging the cardinal rules and tailoring plans to best fit *your* organization extends still further. Challenge crisis management textbooks – all of them. Including the ones I've cited in this handbook. I have a library of books from other experts, and there isn't a single textbook I agree with 100%. There is no question that I have gleaned good information from multiple sources throughout my career, but although some of the key parameters hold up from year to year, others shift and no longer bear repeating.

The concept of a war room is a perfect example. As mentioned earlier, Jane's – back in the day – listed the following supplies for the well-equipped war room:[51] [See section 4.1.2.]

- whiteboards
- televisions
- phones
- hand mirror…

Do you need these items today for *your* organization's crisis deliberations? Do you need a crisis war room at all?

5.7 Rule 7: Nurture Traditional Media Contacts?

Similarly, it is generally considered best practice to build a media contact list, regularly update the contact list, have regular periodic contact with reporters on the contact list, distribute a media guide with your organization's contact information[52] and otherwise build a relationship with your key media contacts. (Again, *who* is setting these rules and why isn't anyone challenging them?)

The average length of tenure for many journalists climbing the ladder from small town to larger demographic and more prestigious news organization, is just a couple of years. Unless you are constantly building and revising this media list, it's never going to be accurate. A better choice might be to have on hand (or contract this information from a service) the main contact information for pertinent news desks for the largest cities in your region as well as the ultra-local news desks. (For this, think in terms of the weekly small-town newspaper for the town your business is located in.) Plan to send news alerts directed at the "news desk" for the news organizations on your list, rather than any specific editor.

It may well be worth trying to nurture media contacts with your town's small-town paper by inviting them to observe drills or attend facility rollouts or community days – so they can see your organization in a positive context. But I have found it next to impossible to realistically expect that an organization will otherwise be able to build and nurture a relationship with top media outlets. Unless you are regularly providing news for them to feed on, they're not going to be interested in covering non-news PR events that amount to free advertising for you.

Instead of nurturing relationships with individual major media reporters, be prepared to have spokespersons available in the event the media need to reach you during a crisis event. Make it *easy* for them to find and reach you.

Ensure contact information is clearly posted on your website and that inquiries will get through to a live person 24/7/365. Voicemail isn't good enough. Make sure that number is transferred to someone's cell phone – even in the middle of the night, and that whoever is manning the number has easy access to all key personnel, no matter the time of day. Even though you may have identified key journalists and nurtured them, it is not certain that those will be the journalists assigned to the story when your crisis breaks. You'll have a lot of new acquaintances knocking on your door, and you'll need to build rapport instantly rather than falling back on an existing relationship.

Summary

Best practices established many years ago may be outdated. This chapter urged you to take a very hard look at some of the best practices of business continuity to determine whether they're truly best practice for *your* organization, or whether there are better practices you can put into play.

Questions for Further Thought and Discussion

> ➤ *What crisis/business continuity cardinal rules have you been relying on without fully challenging? Are there others to add to the list discussed in this chapter?*
> ➤ *Have you set aside an alternate facility for your organization's disaster recovery needs?*
> ➤ *Have you done a formal risk analysis at your organization (where risks have been rated on likelihood as a tool to determine where best to spend mitigation dollars)? If so, how accurate has the analysis been so far?*

CHAPTER 6

WHAT'S YOUR CRISIS DREAM TEAM?

Large companies may have an internal crisis management expert on staff. Smaller companies may believe it's something only large companies have the luxury to do – so they often outsource it to public relations consulting firms that specialize in crisis communications.

That's shortsighted on two counts.

1. Most crisis consulting firms will require a retainer because they want to ensure they've established a relationship and familiarity with the company so that they can jump in running when a crisis hits. But an established relationship with a consulting firm is nowhere near as viable as an on-the-ground expert who is truly embedded in the organization, because they stand a better chance of identifying an escalating potential crisis and *averting* it.
2. Retaining that PR firm is likely going to cost more. Paying outsourced public relations firms to clean up a mess or make it sound not as bad will cost not only in retainer and activation fees but also in terms of lost reputation costs. But what if you'd been

able to avoid the hits to reputation by avoiding the crisis altogether?

Almost all companies seem to think that the crisis management function will handle or respond to crises, when in fact the crisis expert should be preventing them or minimizing them before they happen. Being entirely reactive is rarely a good strategy in business.

This chapter covers:

- *Why to consider internal capability rather than relying on outside resources to step in if/when necessary.*
- *What it takes to create your crisis dream team internally.*
- *Who should be on the team?*
- *Determining when to activate them.*

6.1 Hiring a Firm to Respond Reactively

Actual 2018 job postings focused on reactive crisis management and identifying likely risks:[53]

"... this individual is responsible for Crisis Management response coordination... mitigating the impacts of natural disasters and man-made crises."

"... Coordinate and manage response and recovery efforts in the event of a business disruption... Determine need for activation... during a business disruption based on severity levels or other escalation triggers..."

- "Take a lead role in developing and updating company risk taxonomy
- Drive alignment and coordination across 2nd line of defense using risk taxonomy
- Lead risk champions in implementation of company risk appetite..."

Business resiliency focused on risk analysis and prioritization of the likelihood of identified hazards causing a business disruption, and then resource allocation and business resumption planning to get back in business quickly following an identified disruption event, is not at all the same as crisis avoidance. In fact, in most cases, the crises that derail organizations are not always the events business impact analyses (BIA) and risk studies have prioritized as a high likelihood risk in the first place. Certainly, there is a role for business continuity planning, but that sort of planning is tactical and reactive rather than strategic and proactive.

An organization that has a crisis management team of empowered decisionmakers with a clear structure and process as well as functional leads from HR, Facilities, etc. already in place, is much better prepared than an organization that handles its crisis management ad hoc.

6.2 Who Do We Activate and When Do We Activate?

Without structure and a clear process that is exercised and improved, someone who believes they need to be (or who truly should be) involved can get left out. At best, this results in executives feeling they're out of the loop. It can also turn your crisis avoidance efforts into a misstep or missed opportunities. [See kidnapping example in section 4.1.4.]

Even more important than having a structured crisis team in place and prepared is for the entire leadership team within the organization to know who is on this team (or who their representative is) as well as what types of incidents require reporting and the thresholds for reporting.

Thresholds that identify situations that "have the potential to"

- cost X amount of money
- injure customers, neighbors, or employees
- negatively impact brand or reputation or relationships with stakeholders…

… are better than reactive thresholds that kick in once the identified level has been surpassed.

As mentioned in the previous chapter, it's important to activate the entire team rather than just those who need to know.

It's an element of human nature to hope for the best, hope bad news doesn't get out, hope the boss doesn't hear about your screw-up. On the flip side, bosses want to hear that their advisors believe they don't have to take the hard actions, that they can walk back from the dark edge.

For decades, Catholic church leadership told itself it was okay to self-rehabilitate priests who had abused children, send them away to relearn appropriate behavior, remove them from parishes rather than prosecute them publicly. But it wasn't okay in the court of public opinion. The Catholic sex abuse scandal cost the church millions and tarnished the religion's reputation immeasurably. It was entirely avoidable if church leadership had self-reported the incidents as they happened and assisted the courts to prosecute the priests as sex offenders (instead of harboring and "rehabilitating" or retiring them internally).

The Catholic church should have also put in place corrective actions including educational awareness programs to bring the situation to light, warning altar boys about inappropriate touching, and encouraging them to report it to another adult rather than to face years of shame and self-loathing.

At one of the companies I worked with, I was in the middle of media training executives and had just brought up on the screen an example of how Blue Bell dealt with listeria contamination in its ice cream. [More on this crisis in section 10.2.]

118

One of the business unit presidents turned to one of his counterparts and joked about the timeliness of the example because his business unit was currently dealing with a similar issue!

To his credit, that shocked counterpart told him in no uncertain terms that he needed to call the crisis team together. Until that moment, however, it hadn't occurred to the business unit president to raise the issue to that level because word of the crisis had not yet gotten out.

As it turned out, the business unit president and his leadership team were flummoxed because tests kept coming back indicating E. coli contamination was appearing in their product – even though it was thought to be impossible for this product to incubate E. coli in the first place. Because the business unit leadership team did not know how the E. coli was being introduced and had no idea how far back the contamination went – in other words, because they had not compiled the answers – they had not notified their customers. In their minds, as long as they could find and fix the problem before the customers found out, they stood a chance of avoiding a pretty serious crisis.

Because of the overwhelming inclination to keep the crisis from getting out, they'd confined knowledge of the problem to just a handful of people. But without the resources and input of the broader crisis team, they were covering up instead of working collaboratively with those who could keep the issue from being a crisis. (Because the customers had no indication there was a problem, they were continuing to use the contaminated material as feedstock for their food product – which was still being stocked on grocery shelves nationwide!)

I had the business unit president on the phone with key customers an hour later. Over the course of the next couple of weeks of close collaboration (including the customers and legal teams and their combined product quality and testing laboratories) they were able to not only reexamine end use product to ensure the customers' process had always included steps to kill any E. coli before releasing their product, but also to find and fix the problem. It would be hard to say the clients were pleased to hear about the problem, but they did appreciate that the organization did not take a wait-and-see stance and cross their fingers that it wouldn't become a crisis for their clients before speaking up.

Getting an issue into the hands of the crisis team every time can be a herculean shift in culture, but once the corporate mindset has been adjusted to report rather than to obfuscate, they're on the path to crisis *avoidance* instead of crisis reaction.

In the earlier IT hacking example [see section 4.1.4], the IT department pulled the crisis team together to plan actions even though they were convinced it wasn't really a crisis – more routine than anything else – that the team was being called together just to check the boxes.

It would have been easier to cross fingers and hope we shut the hackers down in time, but not only would that have been shortsighted, it would have led to a loss of confidence if the users' identities were compromised and they didn't find out until after the fact that it had been our fault and we hadn't warned them in time to take preventive action.

6.2.1 Case Study on Waiting and Hoping the Crisis Isn't Discovered – Uber (2016-2017)

Uber – take note. Paying off hackers in 2016 did indeed come to light (in 2017). Customers and drivers weren't angry so much by the fact that Uber had been hacked, since that seems to be commonplace now. They were angriest that Uber tried to cover it up. And Uber rolled out the red carpet for more attacks, now that hackers know they are willing to open their checkbook to pay them off.[54]

Worse was the lack of compassion in Uber's messaging when the incident came to light.[55]

Lesson learned: stakeholders are often angrier that a mistake was covered up than that a mistake was made.

Summary

What is your crisis dream team? How do you build that kind of capability internally rather than relying on consultants to swoop in? This chapter covered determining your team and how to get them in the game.

Questions for Further Thought and Discussion

- *What's your crisis dream team? Do you have an internal team, prepped and ready, or do you rely on a PR firm?*
- *The last time a crisis occurred at your organization, did you activate a select few ad hoc individuals, or the entire crisis team? How did it work out?*
- *Describe a time when you took the opposite approach. How did it work out?*

CHAPTER 7

SIGNAL DETECTION

How does an organization identify a crisis in the incipient stage and head it off?

Speaking up fast and having a team practiced and ready to react isn't enough to manage a crisis well. Is it possible to identify an escalating crisis before it reaches crisis proportions and stop it from getting there? Stopping a crisis *before* it becomes a crisis is the ultimate act of crisis management. But most organizations have no idea how to do this.

Much of the reason for the inability to identify an escalating issue before it reaches a crisis level is because most organizations approach the identification of crisis with a reactive mindset. Thresholds for convening the organization's crisis team often focus on *after* a certain level of damage has occurred. But what if thresholds instead were focused on the *potential* for damage to reputation… the *potential* for media attention… the *potential* for _____ ?

The larger the organization, the harder it can be to identify a circumstance that is escalating and to report it to the right level where leadership and crisis team members can respond quickly. After the fact, it is often easy enough to recognize that there were signals that would have portended that something was derailing, but somehow those signals didn't manage to get to the point where they could be heard by the right people who could have done something about them. The trick is to identify the signal detectors and then increase the volume to the point where they can be heard by the right people.[56]

This chapter covers:

- *How to detect the signals of a potential crisis before the crisis happens.*
- *Identifying signal detectors.*
- *Creating the right environment to increase the chances of hearing the signals.*

7.1 Picking Up on Signals

Let's not overcomplicate this.

In most cases, leaders are not the signal detectors. It's the people who don't think they are authorized to do anything about "it," whatever "it" may be. So first, dissect what it is that you want to hear about. Second, identify who or what the signal detectors may be that are capable or in the right position to be able to hear what is happening. Third, authorize them to channel those signals to the right level where they can be heard and interpreted in context by the right people.

Part of the difficulty is picking up signals in different sectors and putting them together holistically. Crises often happen because multiple events are cascading at once, signaling an organization that is not acting according to its values or public expectations. Singly, any one of the items might not cause a crisis but together signal that an organization may not be acting ethically, that quality assurance is shoddy, that leadership is penny-pinching with regard to safety... and it becomes beyond the public's tolerance.

7.1.1. Coca Cola—Creeping Crisis Case Study (1999)[57]

Timeline:

- June 8, 1999 – School children in Bornem, Belgium become nauseated after drinking Coca-Cola at school. 42 are hospitalized.
- June 10 – Eight children are hospitalized in Bruges, Belgium after drinking Coke and Fanta.
- June 12-14 – A call center for health complaints about Coca-Cola products receives 200 calls.
- June 14 – Forty-two children are hospitalized in Lochristi, Belgium. The government orders all Coca-Cola products off the market.
- June 15 – Luxembourg bans Coca-Cola products. France closes a bottling plant in Dunkirk. The Netherlands bans Coca-Cola products shipped through Belgium.
- June 16 – Coca-Cola issues its first apology to European consumers.
- June 18 – Coca-Cola's chairman Douglas Ivester arrives in Belgium to oversee management of the crisis.
- June 22 – Coca-Cola apologizes to Belgian consumers - Ivester agrees to new precautions at bottling plants.
- June 23 – Belgium lifts its ban.
- June 25 – Other countries lift restrictions.
- June 29 – Recall in Poland. Mold is found growing at the bottom of 1500 bottles of Bonaqua bottled water caused by inadequate washing of returnable bottles.

Analysis of this creeping crisis:

- Breakdown of quality control.
- Missed early warning signs.
- Did not see the big picture.
- Dissemination of bad information leads to loss of consumer confidence and trust.
- Chairman was brought in as spokesman eight days late.

- Ad campaign and expert witnesses (brought in to testify that Coke was safe to drink, when in reality the company didn't really know what caused the problems and wasn't 100% sure that the Coke products *weren't* harmful).
- Recall in Poland brings Coke back to square one.

Rivals step in:

- Coke in China – China is Coke's 6th biggest foreign market. Usually Coca-Cola and Pepsi are about equal in sales, but during the Coke crisis, Pepsi sales in China doubled that of Coke.
- Virgin Cola in Belgium – traditionally held a three percent share of Belgium's soft drink market, compared with Coca-Cola's 86% share. Virgin Cola's production in Belgium ran at about 10 times the normal level in the wake of the Coke crisis.
- Gain for non-soft drinks.

Financial loss:

- Recall of 14 million cases of Coke products in five European countries. It was the biggest product recall in the company's 113-year history.
- 2nd quarter operating profit was shaved by about $35million.
- Share price over the course of the crisis dropped to $61 against a year high of $88. Share price continued to fall steadily until the end of September – when it hit a low of $49.
- On December 6th, Douglas Ivester announced his retirement – after just two years as Chairman/CEO of Coca-Cola.

Lesson learned: creeping crises are often the result not only of multiple failures caused by a lack of attention to values or public expectations, but also an inability to put warning signals in different sectors together holistically.

7.2 Creating the Right Environment

As discussed earlier, the chemical industry is generally ultra-cautious when it comes to safety. They report accidents that most would not consider accidents. It came as a surprise to me the first time I saw a bee sting get reported against the total reportable incident report for the month (even though it was a gardening contractor outside the facility who was stung). Similarly, a maintenance contractor slipped while washing the lavatory floor and that counted against that month's total reportable incident count. In any other industry, many would never have thought to report either incident. But working at a chemical company was a whole different mindset.

And it was drummed into every employee's head. We all went through safety training programs aimed at educating us on slips, trips, and falls as well as behaviors that lead to accidents. These include inattention, rushing, complacency, eyes not on task, mind not on task, being in the line of fire.[58] There were mandatory monthly safety meetings in which we were asked to share any personal examples from the last month. Did we recognize these behaviors in something we were doing and changed course as a result, thereby lessening our chance of accident? We were asked to share because in sharing we could learn from each other.

All this ultra-vigilance led to a culture in which we were expected to speak up if we saw anyone else engaging in unsafe behavior. It was a common occurrence in the laboratories (and even the office environment) to team up to do a behavioral analysis of common tasks – to observe and identify for the person if there was anything they might consider doing safer.

There was an aura of we're-all-in-this-together because the safety record for the site was tied to performance reviews and bonus amounts and therefore impacted us all. If someone was trying to walk down the stairs with an armful of stuff and didn't have a hand free to hold the handrail, anyone who saw the action would chide them (even if that person were their boss) and offer to help them carry whatever they were carrying. Coffee spills in the kitchenette were never just left for someone else to clean up. I took to wearing heavy tread "sensible" shoes rather than heels. Most women did. Former Arkema Americas CEO Bernard Roche made a point of holding a review of any accidents that occurred to better understand how they had occurred and what could be done differently. His motto was "zero is possible."[59]

This mindset of speaking up immediately and having minor incidents treated with great seriousness is the sort of environment that is needed to create signal detection. In this case, the "it" leadership wanted to hear about was any potential near miss that could have become an accident (even if it would have been minor).

The signal detectors capable – or in the right position – to be able to hear what is happening were the employees. Every single one of them – those in the labs, administrative personnel… everyone.

Every person was not only authorized to channel those signals to the right level where they could be heard and interpreted in context by the right people, but encouraged with all seriousness, up through leadership and the CEO.

The result was a marked decrease in major emergencies causing injuries or off-site impacts because of unsafe actions. People didn't gripe that management was just paying lip service to safety concerns. Employees didn't look back and say, "Well, I could have told you that was an accident waiting to happen," because it would have been dishonorable to have let it get that far without whistleblowing or tattling. Essentially, crisis avoidance was a result of signal detectors being everywhere and constantly reporting upwards.

Summary

It is easy – in hindsight – to see how an incident escalated into a crisis. But how do you derail a potential crisis with foresight? This chapter covered how to identify signal detectors within your organization and how to create the right environment for noticing the signals that can harbinger a crisis before the situation takes a turn for the worse.

Questions for Further Thought and Discussion

➢ *Describe a time when your organization was involved in a creeping crisis. How quickly were you able to detect the signals?*

➢ *What role did signal detectors play in that situation?*

➢ *What additional steps can you take at your organization to create an environment that will better ensure the right signal detectors are able to elevate key signals to the right ears?*

CHAPTER 8

APOLOGY AS A BUSINESS DECISION

Apology is about bringing closure to the victim by acknowledging actions of the perpetrator which were hurtful. An apology – done well – can go a long way towards healing a rift and mitigating the possibility of a lawsuit, whereas an apology done badly can pour gas on a flame.

Norwood Teague, on resigning as the University of Minnesota athletic director after two sexual harassment charges:

"[I] had entirely too much to drink" and sent "truly inappropriate texts... I apologize."

It may contain the word apology, but there's no indication Teague meant it. There's no humility, no acknowledgement that a wrong was done against another person nor any acceptance of responsibility. You can't skip these important elements.[60]

Similarly, when actor Kevin Spacey claimed he did not remember an alleged sexual advance claimed by actor Anthony Rapp 30 years earlier when Rapp was 14, Spacey's castaway apology led to widespread criticism from the LGBT community, not only for Spacey's suggestion that drink (not himself) was to blame, but also because he indicated it was a choice to be gay or not and used the excuse of coming out of the closet to address an allegation that he'd made a sexual move on a minor.

"I have loved and had romantic encounters with men throughout my life, and I choose now to live as a gay man." – Kevin Spacey

The backlash left the iconic Netflix "House of Cards" without a lead as the network sought to distance itself with giant steps from the actor and the scandal. (And director Ridley Scott brought in Christopher Plummer a month before "All the Money in the World" opened – to replace and reshoot all of Kevin Spacey's scenes rather than release a film that seemingly condoned the actor's behavior.)[61]

This chapter covers:

- *The attributes of an effective apology.*
- *The role apologies play in perception of fault and legal liability.*
- *Media coverage of apologies.*
- *A formula for apology as a business decision.*

8.1 What is an Appropriate Apology?

There is some variation in what people will accept as an appropriate apology.[62] Although a partial apology may consist of no more than an acknowledgment of responsibility and an expression of remorse,[63] more complete apologies contain an accounting of events, a description of damage, and an offer of reparation.[64] Full-blown apologies contain:

- an apology
- an expression of remorse
- a promise not to repeat the offense
- a request for forgiveness, and
- an offer to provide compensation.[65]

Victims also find full-blown apologies more satisfactory than excuses or justification of actions,[66] with the victim's order of preference usually being full-blown apology, regret plus excuse, apology alone, regret alone, excuse alone, regret plus justification, and justification alone.[67]

8.1.1 Case Study – United Passenger Dragged Off Plane (2017)

Dr. David Dao suffered a serious concussion, broken nose, the loss of two teeth and other injuries when he was dragged off United Flight 3411 at O'Hare Airport after refusing to vacate the seat he paid for and deplane to make room for crew members who needed to be ferried to another airport via the overbooked flight.[68]

Take a look at the video clip:

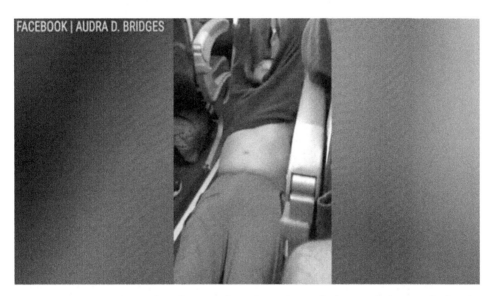

Fig. 8-1. Audra D. Bridges' video of Dr. David Dao being dragged of a United plane can be found at https://www.cnbc.com/2017/04/10/video-surfaces-of-man-being-dragged-from-overbooked-united-flight.html

The incident led to United's CEO acknowledging (via full-page ads) that that was not the way to treat a paying customer, and a promise to change.[69]

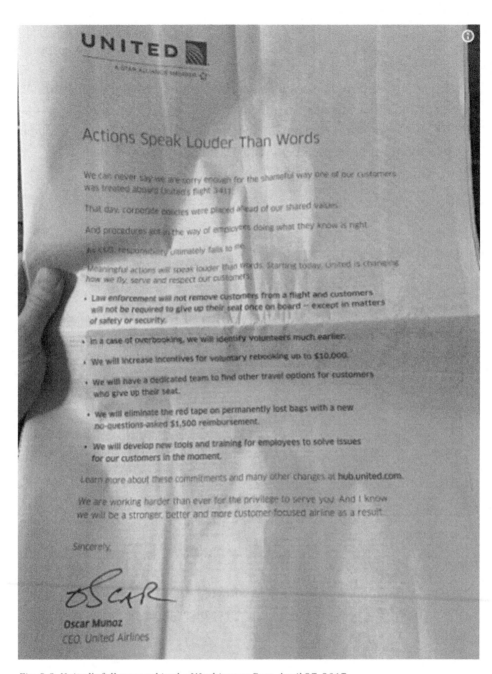

Fig. 8-2. United's full-page ad in the Washington Post, April 27, 2017.

Unfortunately, the missive came after first blaming the victim.[70]

A little common sense could have gone a long way toward preventing the public relations crisis.[71]

Lesson learned: actions speak louder than words. Apologies ring hollow when stakeholders don't believe they are sincerely offered.

8.2 Do You Mean It?

An explanation is more likely to be accepted if there is an expression of repentance and if the victim believes the person who committed the wrong is not likely to commit the offense again.[72] Those who are wronged are often less aggressive in seeking recompense if an apology is offered.[73]

Apologies can be an important resource for tempering antagonisms and resolving conflicts but providing a satisfactory apology can be a delicate transaction. Although it can't undo the wrong, an effective apology can eradicate the consequences by eliciting forgiveness from the wronged party.[74]

The key appears to be whether the hearer believes the apology to be sincere.[75]

Senator Bob Packwood's apology to the women he was accused of sexually harassing while a member of Congress is a good example of an insincere apology: "I'm apologizing for the conduct that it was alleged that I did." Not only was the apology insincere, it failed to acknowledge wrong-doing, and created further resentment.[76]

By proffering a penitential account, the harm-doer can often reduce the victim's negative perceptions as well as reduce the amount of sanctions levied against the harm-doer.[77] Or the obverse can be true.

For example, a series of delivery accidents involving Domino's Pizza drivers who were speeding in order to deliver their pizzas in less than 30 minutes led to a driver's death and public criticism over the Domino's apology literally attached to the top of its pizza boxes. In its pizza box-top statement, Domino's tried to reframe the issue to scapegoat its drivers, explaining that the average pizza only needed to go two miles. What Domino's didn't mention was that each driver may be carrying as many as four pizzas when he/she leaves the store, all of which are expected to be delivered before the half-hour timeframe is up.[78]

Similarly, Exxon attempted to reframe itself as a victim in the Valdez crisis – which Exxon claimed wasn't really its fault but rather the fault of Alaskan officials who refused to allow the company to use the dispersant Corexit 9527 on the slick. Exxon's argument was that "the company attempted to take quick and decisive action, but environmentally inclined bureaucrats hamstrung it." The Exxon apology also tapped into the widely publicized story (spread by Exxon) that Valdez captain Hazelwood was drunk – absolving the company while scapegoating the employee.[79]

Exxon took out a newspaper advertisement apologizing for the spill, but not taking responsibility. Exxon pointed a lot of fingers in different directions – at the Coast Guard and Alaskan officials for failing to allow the dispersant, to Hazelwood for his alleged drunkenness. Exxon's blame-shifting, rather than taking responsibility, was a significant contributor towards the public's rejection of Exxon's apology. One of the strongest criticisms was directed at Chairman and CEO Lawrence Rawl for failing to appear in public for nearly a full week after the tanker ran aground. When he did talk, he tended to blame others.[80]

The Ford-Firestone crisis[81] – in which both companies tried to blame the other – is also an example of blame shifting that backfired and further dragged out bad publicity.

As John Wildgust says in his critique in the journal *Public Relations*, finger-pointing only undermines consumer confidence and prolongs the media-exposure agony. Remedy: One clear statement accepting responsibility would have been less damaging than sustained media hits about tire pressure and public debate about the integrity of the company."[82]

ValuJet CEO Lewis Jordan also sought to downplay the company's accident-prone record and scapegoat subcontractor Sabretech (which packed, labeled, and delivered five boxes of oxygen generators incorrectly) as the cause of its fatal crash into the Florida Everglades. His argument was that there would not have been a crash if Sabretech had done its job. ValuJet knew that to gain governmental approval and win back its customers, it had to reassure its stakeholders of its commitment to safety, but its claims weren't persuasive enough in the context of its bare-bones maintenance and service policies and its large profit margins. Additionally, ValuJet never voluntarily accepted responsibility for the crash itself, or made a heartfelt apology.[83]

The downside to accepting responsibility, of course, is the potentially high financial costs. However, if an organization is at fault, it can repair its reputation much faster if it apologizes, accepts responsibility, and shows remorse.[84] Attempts to shift the blame can backfire and hinder further public relations efforts.[85]

8.2.1 Case Study on the Unconvincing Apology – Lululemon (2013)

In 2013, yoga pant maker Lululemon drew heat when embarrassed customers started noticing that the pants they were wearing in public were so sheer they were practically see-through. Founder Chip Wilson offered an apology that was so egotistical it put the blame on the customers themselves!

Fig. 8-3. Lululemon's victim-blaming apology can be found at
http://www.youtube.com/watch?v=u4jIBlTIkSk

Lesson learned: apologies that put the blame on the victim are unconvincing non-apologies. Save your breath.

8.3 Legal Liability

Incorporating more apologies when warranted could significantly reduce punitive damage awards.[86] So why then, isn't apology usually considered a first option for crisis communicators?

Even in the face of overwhelming evidence, some organizations deny wrongdoing because of the fear that admitting responsibility could be used against them in court.[87] The legal logic to this is that, if you apologize, then you have admitted wrongdoing or dereliction of duty. It can be an ongoing conflict between the advice offered by a company's public relations practitioners and its lawyers. While the public relations practitioners advise "openness," the lawyers advise "no comment" and it can be a challenge to find middle ground between the two disciplines.[88] From the attorney's viewpoint, it doesn't really matter what the public thinks as long as the case is won; and from the public relations viewpoint, if the public is persuaded of the rightness of the decision-maker's goals,

138

public opinion will pull all else with it – including the court of judicial opinion.[89]

But can the two teams work together as one to encourage apology in the interests of derailing the conflict?

There is a good deal of anecdotal evidence to suggest that in many cases injured parties would never have brought suit (or would have dropped their suit) if the offender had just apologized. It creates a cycle in which an offender who may want to apologize doesn't do so because of the fear of lawsuit, yet it is the absence of apology that continues to drive the lawsuit.[90]

8.4 Paying Costs

One tactic for attempting to side-step responsibility has been to pay for the damage to victims, without acknowledging blame or otherwise apologizing.

For example, when people became ill during its E. coli crisis, Jack in the Box offered to pay hospital costs regardless of whether the victims intended to take legal action. However, the company qualified the payments on a case-by-case basis after determining whether the patients were linked to the E. coli poisoning attributed to Jack in the Box or whether they were "simply one of the nearly 200 cases of E. coli that occur every year in Washington [state] alone unrelated to our restaurants."[91]

Like Jack in the Box, Odwalla (also struck by an E. coli crisis) expressed concern for the victims and offered to pay medical expenses, but only the medical bills of victims who could prove Odwalla had caused their illness. While it accepted responsibility for the problem, Odwalla simultaneously attempted to limit its responsibility for reparations.[92]

In contrast, when forty McDonald's customers were shot by a gunman in San Diego, CA in 1984, the company's legal staff professed to be more concerned with ensuring the victims were taken care of than worrying about lawsuits. McDonald's general counsel purportedly told those responding to media calls not to worry about the legal implications, just "do what's right for the survivors and families of the victims and we'll worry about the lawsuits later."[93]

In this same vein, Swissair made immediate payments to the families of the victims of its 1998 crash – to assist them in covering the costs of travel, funerals, and lost work.[94] Similarly, when a flawed tank at Ashland Oil collapsed in 1988, one of the key things Ashland officials did to quickly demonstrate acceptance of responsibility and engender good will was to reimburse claims from the start rather than waiting for liability to be established. Advance payments went to the Audubon Society, Bird Rescue, the Red Cross, local volunteer fire departments and others to pay for up-front costs of cleaning up the spill. Ashland even solicited claims from those evacuated – by writing a letter offering to reimburse hotel and meal expenses as well as an additional $200 to compensate them for the inconvenience. Ashland stock lost approximately $3.50 after the spill but was back to its pre-spill level ($57) within a month, and by the time the stock split later in the year, it had risen above $72 a share.[95]

Regardless of whether the company is ready to shoulder responsibility or apologize, public relations experts agree that it is important to at least be empathetic. By showing concern and presenting a human face, stakeholders are more likely to think of the organization as trustworthy; whereas pointing fingers and assigning blame are associated with defensiveness and guilt. John Hall, Ashland Oil's chairman and CEO, advised, "If the public perceives you are truly sorry and that you genuinely want to do the right thing, they will usually forgive you rather quickly."[96]

8.5 Early Apology

If an apology is to be employed, it should be employed quickly.[97]

Early apologies can help defuse anger and prevent an injury from turning into a legal dispute in the first place.

According to the research of J.R. Cohen in his *Southern California Law Review* article "Advising Clients to Apologize" and D. L. Levi's *New York University Law Review* article "The Role of Apology in Mediation," apologies can go a long way toward lessening anger and also legal litigation. "If, soon after an injury, the injured party receives an apology, the bitterness of not receiving an apology may never set in, and the injured party may never bring a legal claim. By subtracting the insult from the injury through apology, litigation can often be avoided... Failing to apologize following an injury can be a deeply disrespectful act and thus become a second injury."[98]

Apologies work best when there aren't priors undermining the sincerity of what is being apologized for. The more times an apology is needed, the less each successive apology rings true, since that would seem to demonstrate that the company's past attempts to correct the problem or problems have been less than sincere.[99] [See Chipotle case study in section 2.5.1 and Taco Bell case study in section 2.3.3.]

Since the public is usually more willing to forgive an organization with a positive performance history than an organization with a history of problems,[100] organizations with negative performance histories can especially benefit from sincere and quick mea culpas that also detail appropriate steps that have been taken to ensure the situation won't happen yet again.[101] When evidence against the company is strong and blame cannot easily be shifted because a similar situation has happened before and the public has lost trust, pledging corrective action may be much more important than attempting to minimize legal liability.[102]

8.5.1 Case Study – Not Early or Quick – Equifax (2017)

It wasn't the first time consumer credit and personally identifying information was compromised because of a hacking (<u>Anthem 2015</u>[103], <u>Office of Personnel Management (OPM) 2015</u>[104]...) and it certainly won't be the last. But why aren't these organizations learning from each other's mistakes?

In 2017, criminals hacked into most of credit-rating agency Equifax's massive dossier. Then Equifax neglected to tell those who had been hacked for several weeks. Once Equifax did admit the breach, it refused to answer questions about the strength (or lack) of its security system. It came out later that they had failed to apply a security patch, and that was the method the hackers had used to undermine the company's security. Making the breach even more egregious: consumers whose information was compromised never had the option to opt out of the credit agency's "services." Although Equifax eventually offered the ability for individuals to "lock" their credit information, it necessitated the need for those whose information had been stolen to pay for the other credit agencies to lock their stolen information.[105]

Lesson learned: regardless of whether they are at fault, companies in crisis should still seek to embrace the following two strategies:

1. An immediate statement of regret or concern for victims (even when liability concerns may preclude a direct statement of responsibility).
2. A strategy of corrective action, in which the organization describes what it plans to do to ensure that the situation never arises again in the future.[106]

8.6 Japanese Apology

Research into the differences between American and Japanese styles of apology have found significant differences in the use of apology, media strategies, and litigation concerns.

Japanese apologies include statements of remorse more often than U.S. apologies. Not only do the Japanese tend to apologize more often than Americans, their apologies are often more robust.[107] In Japan, apology is considered to be an integral part of conflict resolution, whereas U.S. litigants are more likely to consider paying the damages rather than offering an apology. In Japanese courts, the lack of apology is more likely to result in heavy punishment.[108]

In their article "The Implications of Apology: Law and Culture in Japan and the United States" in *Law & Society Review*, Hiroshi Wagatsuma and Arthur Rosett discuss the differences between Japanese apologies and American apologies. "Japanese apologize by acknowledging their fault, while Americans believe that a statement of explanation or justification of their behavior is an appropriate apology. Many Japanese seem to think it is better to apologize even when the other party is at fault, while Americans may blame others even when they know they are at least partially at fault… An apology in the Japanese cultural context is an indication of an individual's wish to maintain or restore a positive relationship with another person."[109]

"In Japan it is believed that the settlement of any amount of compensation will go smoothly if both parties start out apologizing to each other. This insight – that apology is an important ingredient in resolving conflict – is hardly unique to the Japanese. It is something every eight-year-old knows, yet somehow it tends to be swallowed up during adult American discussions of law and business."[110]

Anecdotal evidence would seem to indicate that offering a Japanese-style full apology could in the long run be less costly in many instances than the more cautious traditional American approach. For example, a 1985 Dallas Morning News article highlighted the litigation costs surrounding two similar airplane crashes – one Japanese and one filled with American passengers. The article claimed there were 60 lawsuits filed in the United States after an Air Canada jet flying from Dallas to Toronto caught fire in 1983 and killed 23 passengers.

By contrast, a 1982 Japan Airlines (JAL) crash which killed 24 passengers (and which was officially blamed on a JAL pilot with a history of mental problems) resulted in no lawsuits. The difference in approach was that JAL's president visited the families of most of the crash victims, offered sympathy, apologized, paid homage and extended a monetary settlement of what was reported to be $400,000 for each victim.[111]

It would stand to reason that positively influencing the public's perceptions prior to a court decision may positively influence the court's determination of liability and punitive damages. From a financial standpoint, it is possible that apology that positively influences public perception could be beneficial even with the risk that an admission of guilt could bring, because the consequences of the determination of guilt are at least partially ameliorated by the apology itself.

8.7 The Role of Media Coverage

For ongoing crises, an apology can help to decrease the amount of subsequent news coverage, and certainly help to quiet the storm on social media.

Seventy-one percent of journalists surveyed[112] said that an apology would have no effect on the way they portrayed the company – and that their personal opinions about a company's truthfulness would not impact the objectivity of their stories. (One journalist made the distinction that it is a journalist's job to report not to editorialize.)

However, the perceived sincerity of the apology may have a bearing on whether additional news stories are generated. Although more than half (59 percent) of journalists said their assessment of the sincerity of the company's apology would not impact the tone of the subsequent stories they broadcast or published, many admitted if they didn't believe the apology to be sincere their skepticism would make them more apt to dig

144

deeper for additional damaging information and to prolong the story as they continued to publish or broadcast additional news stories about the crisis.

When asked how they determined whether an apology was sincere, the most common responses included:

- Apologies that were given quickly.
- The company showed a willingness to take responsibility.
- The company made efforts to correct the problem rather than just to give a lip service apology with no action to back it.
- Whether the journalist sensed "spin" rather than genuine contrition in the apology.

Media attention following a sincere apology is less damaging than media attention focused on companies that have not apologized. Half of journalists surveyed[113] indicated that the longer the delay, the less sincere they believed the apology to be. This would indicate that offering a sincere apology quickly can lessen the amount of negative media attention. Apologies generate an increase in coverage initially, but then coverage quickly dies off – often to levels lower than the amount of coverage preceding the apology. This could well be because there is no longer a controversy over whether the company will take responsibility.

There is also evidence that companies that apologize are likely to recover market value quicker than those that don't apologize. Most of the companies researched[114] tended to regain market share within a year of the crisis genesis; whereas companies for which no apology was proffered remained flat or dropped lower in stock value. This is an important finding for companies whose stock value and reputation is more important than the possible costs of legal action.

8.8 Apology as a Business Strategy

It is possible that the ability to recover market value quickly can offset court-imposed sanctions resulting from an apology and the acceptance of responsibility. But smaller organizations may not be able to employ this strategy in a blanket fashion, especially in cases where blame is borderline.

The use of apology may be conditional – depending on whether the cost of litigation is likely to be higher than the financial sanctions wrought by reputational damage. For smaller companies in niche markets where customer choice of vendors is limited and in cases where the culpability is not clear, the cost of potential litigation may outweigh the potential loss of customers. However, for larger companies with high stock value and reputation, apology may be a choice worth considering.

Perhaps a simplified formula from a solely financial standpoint would be to determine the difference in stock value. For companies that don't apologize, stock price tends to slope downwards for the first several months then remain fairly stable at the lower rate for the next several months. The stock of companies that apologize tends to trend upwards to reach pre-crisis levels within a year after the apology. By comparing the difference in company value from one extreme to the other, a company can get a rough "apology value." If the potential apology value is equal to or greater than the anticipated cost of court sanctions and legal fees, then a pre-trial apology may be a viable business option.[115]

Questions for Further Thought and Discussion

> *Describe a situation where your organization offered an apology. How would you characterize the apology? Was it sincere? Unconvincing? Did it blame the victim? Was it offered early? Did your lawyers caution against it to protect against legal liability? Did you offer reparations (before ordered to do so by a court of law)?*

> *What was the media's reaction to the apology? Is there anything you would consider doing differently if you had the situation to do over?*

> *Please do the calculation in the last paragraph above to determine the rough apology value (loss of, say, 3% value for the year vs. anticipated cost of court sanctions).*

8.9 Exercise: Brown's Independent Bar

In Coventry England, a little corner bar called Browns Independent Bar, which had a policy of prohibiting soldiers in uniform so as not to intimidate other patrons, walked itself into a boycott after turning away grieving soldiers who dropped in for a pint before acting as pall bearers at the funeral of their friend who had died in Afghanistan.

#BoycottBrowns trended for days on Twitter and 82,000+ people joined the "Boycott Browns in Coventry" group on Facebook.[116]

It led Browns Bar's owner to attempt this pathetic insincere apology:

Fig. 8-4. Brown's Bar offers an insincere apology at http://vimeo.com/44816688

Questions for further thought and discussion

> *Do you consider the apology to be sincere? How do your impressions on the sincerity of the apology color your thoughts about how well the apology was received? If you were Brown's Bar's owner, what could you have done differently to make your apology more sincere?*

➢ *Without sincerity, do you think it will make a difference to get the apology out quickly? Or to offer reparations to the patrons who were refused?*

➢ *Rescript the apology to be more effective.*

Summary

Done right, an apology can dissipate anger and lead to fewer lawsuits. This chapter covered the attributes of an effective apology, the role apologies play in perception of fault and legal liability, insight into media coverage of apologies, and a formula for apology as a business decision.

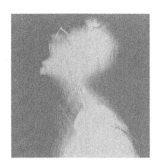

CHAPTER 9

MEDIA TRAINING

When I am engaged 100% in a conversation, I don't blink and apparently people find this very disconcerting.

I use this by way of explanation that it would be a disservice to you to lead you to believe that reading through the information in this chapter is the equivalent of face-to-face media training. It is not.

I was made aware of my non-blinking quirk because of feedback – from interviewees who were a bit creeped out by my intense gaze. Reading all the manuals in the world never would have keyed me in. As with everything else in this book, please consider the information in this chapter supplemental to live training where you are expected to practice what is learned.

This chapter covers:

- *Pitfalls for spokespersons.*
- *Dos and don'ts.*
- *What not to wear.*

9.1 Pitfalls for Spokespersons

9.1.1 Jargon

Do not use technical language that is hard for the ordinary person to understand.[117]

Most reporters are general assignment reporters rather than "beat" reporters or specialists in your industry (trade publications are an exception.) When I was a journalist, the assignment desk would inform me what story or event I'd cover and while the photographer drove to the location, I'd have the length of the car ride to read up on what was known so far and prepare my questions. That's it.

People use jargon unconsciously because they are so used to using the words but also – let's be honest – because they want to appear smart. Being interviewed can be pretty nerve-wracking and the interviewee wants to come off as intelligent. What better way to do that then to use industry jargon to show one is in the know?

Unfortunately, because most reporters don't know the business as well as the interviewee, they're likely to misunderstand or get some of what the interviewee is trying to communicate wrong. Unintentionally. Cut the jargon and increase your chances of communicating what you are trying to get across.

9.1.2 Refute Negative Allegations Without Repeating Them

Don't let a reporter put words in your mouth. Rephrase your answer using words that are not as inflammatory as the reporter's question.[118]

Journalists are skeptical by nature and by training. You can expect to be challenged and have the veracity of what you are saying tested. In many cases, other interviewees have provided other viewpoints that may conflict with yours. Also, traditional journalists are challenged by their editors to get "both" sides of the story. They will often walk into an interview knowing the soundbite or piece of information they'd like to get from you, and rarely will that be the soundbite you want to be

150

recorded giving. They want you to frame the issue in black and white, so the story is point-counterpoint. So they'll try to put words in your mouth. Often framing what they want you to say in negative wording.

Don't bite. Don't repeat the negative wording. With sincere patience, reframe the wording (and premise) as necessary.

For example, following Arkema's Crosby TX crisis in 2017 [see Chapter 3], CEO Rich Rowe was queried about why Arkema was dragging its feet on releasing its Tier II inventory. Houston Chronicle reporter Matt Dempsey's clear implication was that there was a "cover up" of pertinent information about hazardous onsite chemicals the public needed to know about. Instead of acknowledging or repeating the negative "cover-up" wording, Rowe did his best to explain the steps the company was taking to provide the information.

Arkema CEO Rich Rowe: "Why won't we share our Tier II inventory?... As of this morning, we've posted on our website the names of the chemicals that we have at Crosby... I know, that this is not the same as posting the Tier II reports. And there are good reasons for that. To state the obvious, we have dangerous chemicals at the Crosby site. We want to give the information that the public needs to feel and be safe. But we need to keep the more detailed information, for example, the precise quantity and the location of these chemicals from those that would do us harm. That said, we've shared every detail of our Tier II inventory with the people who are responsible for making decisions about public safety. Those are the federal, state, and local emergency response teams, and that led to the imposition of the 1.5-mile evacuation radius which Arkema fully supports."

The answer wasn't what Dempsey wanted to hear and it didn't fit neatly into his point-counterpoint story, so he tried again. VP of Manufacturing Daryl Roberts provided an even more specific answer. Rather than beating around the bush about why the company wasn't willing to provide specific quantities and locations of its (now posted list of) hazardous chemicals, Roberts explained that the reason was because he didn't want to draw a roadmap for potential terrorists.

Reporter: "If you can tell us the components of your Tier II chemicals, why can't you just tell us what they are and the quantities?"

Arkema VP Manufacturing Daryl Roberts: "On the website we have posted exactly what they are. The full list of our Tier II chemicals has been posted. The only information that we have not posted is the exact amount and locations within the site... It was for security reasons from a terrorism standpoint, so we do not want to take the step of providing exact volumes and pinpoint exactly where those things are on the site. That was a policy that was established from a regulatory standpoint and I'll let the regulators take the lead on if they want to change that policy but we don't want to take the lead of making a decision for them."

When quizzed on the toxicity of the smoke coming from the fires, Arkema Business Unit President Rich Rennard took too long to get to the point as he struggled not to use the negative "toxic" wording the reporters were trying to get him to use to characterize the smoke. (This can be tough!) Kudos to him for not repeating the negative wording, *but* his roundabout answer left reporters confused, which in turn led them to ask the same clarifying question repeatedly over the next couple of days. Just as bad.

Reporter: "Is the smoke toxic?"

BU President Rich Rennard: "Certainly this was a fire. And with any fire there is ash and that ash is ultimately going to fall out of the sky and land on the ground. So what we're doing, and instructing residents to do is, if they see any debris or ash that falls onto their property, we would encourage them to call our hotline, and then we will send a team of people out to remove that debris from their property."

Reporter: "Should they consider that ash to be more dangerous than something from a campfire or normal fire?"

Rennard: "It's debris that would be similar to a house fire... When these materials were burning they were inside these trailers and the trailers were made out of... materials. The product was packaged in plastic so there's going to be plastic, trailers and rubber tires on them. Those tires burned. There's insulation on the inside of the trailers, that burns. So that's the kind of combustible materials that would typically be found in that kind of ash."

One more example of reporters trying to put words in the spokesperson's mouth. Sometimes they'll try to put the spokesperson in the quandary of trying to justify the seemingly unjustifiable. In the aftermath of the Crosby crisis, as neighbors within a mile and half were still displaced and more explosions were expected, a reporter asked the CEO whether Arkema is a good neighbor. He could have said "yes" – and that's what the reporter was undoubtedly expecting, but it would have rung hollow. Again, that's the impact the reporter was going for.

Be careful you don't step into this putting-words-in-your-mouth trap either. Especially when a situation is inflammatory and not as black and white as a yes or no answer, take a moment to provide a more thoughtful response. Rather than answering the question, CEO Rich Rowe reframed in his own more positive words and with explanation.

Reporter: "What do you say to people who simply do not trust you to operate safely in their community?"

CEO Rich Rowe: "I would say we've been in the community for a long time. We try to build relationships with the members of that community so that there's a strong relationship that hopefully over time builds trust. We don't have a perfect record. We understand that. We strive to get better at every turn and we'll continue to do so and we hope that through how we handle experiences and matters like this that the perception of the community will only get better."

9.1.3 Do Not Guess if it is Outside Your Area of Expertise[119]

Spokespersons should be knowledgeable, not figureheads. There may be strategic reasons why an organization will choose the spokesperson it chooses. In the most serious of events, the CEO may be the right spokesperson because it lends a sense that the organization understands the gravitas of what has occurred and that leadership has its full attention on the event and is taking personal interest in making sure the situation is handled correctly.

But when technical questions are the focus of the questioning, spokespersons who have the best understanding of the right answers should be the ones answering. If you are the spokesperson and the questioning strays outside your area of expertise, don't guess at the answers (you may get it wrong). Have subject matter experts nearby ready to step up to the mic or promise the reporter you'll get the answer and get back to them.

9.1.4 Keep Answers Short[120]

When I do media training, the number one thing trainees express is "Why bother? The media is just going to take my answers out of context no matter what I do."

Unscrupulous ones will. Most traditionally trained journalists won't.

Here's how you can better ensure you maintain control over what soundbite they choose and whether they need to edit it.

First, if they are successfully able to push your buttons and you respond off the cuff or with anger, anything you say that is jarring or inflammatory will be their first choice. If, on the other hand, you stick with your talking points and messages (covered in the next chapter), it really won't matter which soundbite they use. Just be sure to keep your answers to no more than 20 seconds long.

When I was a TV news journalist, the typical taped story would last about a minute and a half with an anchor intro on the front and a quick one-sentence tag on the end. I had to cram reporter explanation of what had happened along with video of the event/scene/fire raging, and multiple viewpoints (from the fire chief, the next-door neighbor, and also the company spokesperson) into that minute and a half story. The fact is, that's all the time I was allotted. Each element could last only about 10-20 seconds or I wouldn't get it all in. If the spokesperson's best answer lasted longer than 10-20 seconds, I had to cut it short, doing my best to trim out the superfluous.

If your answers to a reporter's questions are self-contained gems that last no more than 20 seconds each (no more than three quick sentences), it won't matter which answer the reporter chooses to use. They'll be able to use it in total, without editing it out of context. You need to edit yourself so they don't have to.

9.1.5 Never Speak Badly of the Other Side[121]

Especially in the early stages of a crisis when the details are still sketchy. It's easy to cast blame away from your organization and scapegoat another party, but don't take the bait. It's so much better to take the high road and say, "It is too early to know who is at fault for the accident. We're working cooperatively with authorities to help them figure out what happened and put in place corrective actions."

9.1.6 Don't Assume the Reporter Has it Right

Most reporters are general assignment reporters[122]. This goes hand-in-hand with not using jargon for the same reason. General assignment reporters don't necessarily have a firm baseline of understanding of the topic, issue, or your industry, and may be struggling to hold an intelligent line of questioning in some cases. Beat reporters cover the same topic (City Hall, for example, or health news) day in and day out and know the terminology and the players. General assignment reporters, by contrast, cover whatever story is assigned to them, regardless of whether they have any knowledge of the subject.

It might be worth your while to educate them. Before the interview begins – as the camera is being set up – there's nothing wrong with giving the interviewer a little bit of basic background so they can ask intelligent questions.

"Before we begin, would it be helpful if I provided you with a quick overview of the site and the products we make here, along with what they are used for?"

Even if that isn't an option, and it is clear the reporter – through ignorance – is stepping into a hole, don't let them fall on their face and look bad in front of their audience. Certainly, there are many spokespersons who might privately cheer when they believe the reporter is looking like an ignoramus, but the appearance of gloating is rarely going to make anyone look good. Gently pull them back on course with a tame correction. After all, you don't want them to get it wrong with misinformation.

Again, using the Arkema Crosby crisis as an example, company spokesperson Daryl Roberts gently corrected the reporter's use of the wrong chemical:

Reporter: "How far are the other chemicals from the organic peroxides, specifically the sulfur dioxide and isobutylene?"

VP of Manufacturing Daryl Roberts: "I don't have the exact number. The two chemicals I think that you are referencing are the [risk management plan] chemicals?"

Reporter: "Yeah."

Roberts: "Isoamylene is near the front of the plant. These [organic peroxide] materials are near the backside of the plant. [sulfur dioxide] is somewhat in the middle. So I would say it would be hundreds of yards and significantly more than that for isoamylene."

9.1.7 Don't Accept Hypothetical Questions

"What if…?"[123]

Answers to hypothetical questions (or any question that begins with "what if") beg for a guess. Don't guess; you might guess wrong. Instead, point out that it is a hypothetical question, that you don't want to guess at answers and bridge [more on bridging in the next chapter—see section 10.6] instead to something you can concretely answer.

Q: "What if neighbors get cancer in 10 years as a result of the toxins you released into the community during today's accident?"

A: "I wouldn't want to guess what will happen in 10 years, but I can tell you what we are doing today to ensure those impacted are being taken care of." [And then elaborate.]

9.1.8 Break Down Multiple Part Questions

If the reporter asks several questions at once, don't try to answer all of them. Choose only one question to answer.[124]

Often this happens in a press conference situation when there are more journalists than scheduled time and they all know the spokesperson won't have the time to circle back around to allow every journalist an opportunity to ask all the questions they'd like answered. So, when called on, the journalist may blurt out all the questions they've got at once and hope the spokesperson answers each question.

If you are the spokesperson, just pick the last question because it will usually be freshest (or if there's a softball question in the middle, go ahead and grab that one instead). Don't make any big deal about choosing only one question and don't point out that the reporter asked multiple questions. There's no point in a preamble to just answering one. Just answer one, then quickly call on the next reporter.

It is not in your best interests to answer all the questions because you may not be able to remember every question. Trying to do so will not only seem stuttering and awkward but could set you up for an inadvertent stumble. When trying to remember, many people tend to look up to the corner of the room, as if they're looking back into their brain for what question they're trying to remember. Unfortunately, that's the same thing most people do when they are lying (and are trying to remember the plausible tale they were going to tell). Without intending to, your body language may leave your audience believing that you've just been less than truthful.

I guarantee that, if any of the others in the string of questions were worthwhile, you won't have to remember them because the next journalist will pick up on it and ask it as their own. "But what about…?" If so, simply answer the now freshly asked repeat. No need to remember it any longer.

9.1.9 Don't Say "No Comment"

It looks like you have something to hide. Explain *why* you can't answer.[125]

This is easier to explain to US audiences who are familiar with the 5th Amendment right to avoid self-incrimination. It's an answer lawyers may coach their clients to say when facing a court battle and they don't want the client to say something incriminating.

But it is neither sufficient nor appropriate for a spokesperson; avoid saying it. Instead, explain why you can't answer. ("The case is in court and we want to ensure due process... or... I am not a subject matter expert on that issue and don't want to provide an incorrect answer...") After explaining why you can't answer, you may also want to consider bridging to something you *can* talk about instead so it doesn't appear you are just deflecting.

9.1.10 Remember Who You are Speaking To When You are Speaking Through the Media[126]

Whenever you are talking to the media, you may be talking to reporters, but your real audience is your customers, those who have been directly impacted by the crisis, regulators, etc. Talk *through* the media to the stakeholders you are actually trying to reach. Because the media act as a filter for your message, it is always best to try to speak to your key audiences as directly as possible. But when you do need to speak through the media, keep in mind who you are really talking to. When the media attempt to push your buttons, ignore the button pushing and speak civilly, treat the questions (and questioners) respectfully the way you'd speak with the audiences you are trying to reach.

9.1.11 Exercise: University Accused of Lying to Hide Killing[127]

Again, there's no substitute for face-to-face practice for media interviews, but try this out anyway. Put yourself in the shoes of the Eastern Michigan University spokesperson who is facing a press conference to respond to the actions the university took following the death of one of its students.

Answer the questions one by one. Take a moment before answering to try to determine which pitfall you might fall in if you aren't vigilant with your answer. Then do your best at answering (in three sentences).

Short synopsis:

- Janitor found Laura Dickinson dead in her Eastern Michigan University dorm room in December.
- Pillow over her face, naked below the waist, door was locked, her keys were gone.
- University said no foul play was suspected.
- University stuck to their story that no foul play was suspected for more than two months – even after they learned the medical examiner had found semen on her body and even as police questioned other students and faculty – and took DNA samples leading to the arrest of a fellow student on rape and homicide charges.
- Now an independent report contends university officials covered up information indicating a crime had been committed.
- The university board accused school authorities of withholding information, deceiving the public, and potentially violating a federal law designed to warn students of campus safety threats.
- *"After they realized they had a murder, not only did they not warn people, they lied about it."* (S. Daniel Carter, SVP Security on Campus)

(You can click on the link to http://www.washingtonpost.com/wp-dyn/content/article/2007/06/20/AR2007062002172.html to read the story.)

QUESTIONS

[You are the spokesperson for the university, which has been criticized into a defensive posture. Pause and take a crack at answering each question *before* reading the feedback.]

> *Reporter: SVP Daniel Carter of the nonprofit organization Security on Campus says not only did you not warn other students of the murder, you lied about it. Why did you lie about it?*

{Feedback: Refute negative allegations without repeating them. The reporter is trying to bait you. Don't take the bait and don't use the word "lie" in your answer. Even if you contend you did not lie about it, you've been backed into a corner of trying to justify your answer when the reporter clearly has someone else who is going to appear more credible as counterpoint. Explain what happened as sincerely as possible.}

> *Do you think this is a situation of too little too late with the best course of action easier seen in hindsight?*

{Feedback: Refute negative allegations without repeating them. It's catchy and concise and easily repeatable. Don't justify your actions. It will appear trite – as if you are not taking accountability and just trying to pass the buck. Be humble. Admit your mistake. Promise to learn from your mistake and make sure you enact change so that this will never happen again. Then make good on that promise.}

> *What is your personal opinion – do you think this is reflective of a campus culture that would rather keep things secret and deal with problems internally?*

{Feedback: Do not guess if it is outside your area of expertise. This is a tough one. You are the spokesperson, which puts you in a tough position: You're supposed to be the mouthpiece for your organization rather than providing your personal opinions. Reporters like to play one off the other in an effort to get you to recognize that whatever your organization did was not empathetic. Most coaches would recommend you stick to the script and answer as the voice for your organization.

Sometimes I've found it is possible to humanize the organization if you can truthfully speak from not only your value system but the organization's. ("We don't believe that.") However, this kind of question is asked specifically because the reporter believes there is a high likelihood your personal standpoint is going to be different from the answer you know your organization would give. Don't give an answer that will ring hollow. Acknowledge that there may be steps your organization can take to improve, then put those steps in action.}

> *Would you say mistakes were made on your watch?*

{Feedback: Refute negative allegations without repeating them. Don't let the reporter put words in your mouth. Don't repeat negative and don't repeat catchy and repeatable phrases. How would *you* explain what went wrong?}

> *A federal law requires universities to publicize crimes on campus and warn students about safety threats. It's called the Clemmons law. Would this be a violation of the Clemmons law?*

{Feedback: Don't assume the reporter has it right. Most reporters are general assignment reporters and won't necessarily have a firm grasp on the technical aspects of the story. It's not the Clemmons law, it's the Cleary Act. Gently correct so the reporter doesn't look like a fool in front of their audience by perpetuating misinformation that makes them look ill-informed. Set them straight as respectfully as you can.}

> *What is the rationale investigators are giving for the two-month delay in reporting this as a homicide investigation?*

{Feedback: Do not guess if it is outside your area of expertise. You are representing the university. Let the investigators represent themselves. Don't put words in their mouths.}

> *What are the legal ramifications likely to be as a result?*

{Feedback: Do not guess if it is outside your area of expertise. Are you a lawyer? If not, don't try to interpret the legal ramifications. You are likely to get it wrong. Simply state, "I'm not a lawyer, so I wouldn't want to guess."}

> *The family says this is really the fault of the police investigation, rather than the university. Would you agree that those in charge of the police investigation should be put on a leave of absence for their incompetence?*

{Feedback: Never speak badly of the other side. When you are under fire, it can be easy to grab a lifeline that is offered. Don't take the bait. Speak with grace and don't scapegoat someone else to try to get the heat off yourself. ("We're working cooperatively to try to set this right.")}

> *According to the victim's roommate, she was often known to misplace her keys. Could this have been a possible reason why the fact that her keys were missing from the room was not given much weight initially?*

{Feedback: Don't accept hypothetical questions. Hypothetical questions ask "what if." The fact is, you don't really know the answer to this – it would just be a guess. You can answer any hypothetical question with "I wouldn't want to guess."}

> *How long will the Vice President for Student Affairs remain on paid leave as a result of this incident?... Why wasn't his pay suspended?... Is this really just meant to be a slap on the wrist?... What do you say about the allegations that the university is making him a scapegoat?*

{Feedback: When you are barraged by a long string of questions from one reporter, don't try to remember all the questions. Choose the last question because it will be the easiest to remember (or any softball question that caught your attention in the middle) and answer just that one question. Then stop speaking and call on the next reporter.}

9.1.12 Exercise: Wyeth Accused of Secret Recall[128]

Let's try this with another scenario. Put yourself in the shoes of the company spokesperson who is facing a press conference to respond to the actions the company took.

Answer the questions one by one. Take a moment before answering to try to determine which pitfall you might fall in if you aren't vigilant with your answer. Then do your best at answering. Again, remember to strive for three sentence answers (no more than 20 seconds each). Were you able to do that with the last set of answers or did you ramble and cause the reporter to have to choose which part of your answer to edit out? This time see if you can make your answers even shorter.

Short synopsis:

- Philippine government is accusing Wyeth of a secret product recall of its infant formula.
- They allege Wyeth removed and destroyed batches of infant formula that had rust on the cans without telling the government or alerting the public.
- FDA says Wyeth only notified them after it had already posted the information on the Internet.
- Wyeth says there was no reason to inform the FDA because the rust was only on the packaging – not in the formula.
- Wyeth destroyed the rusty cans that were recalled even though they say the recall was for "cosmetic reasons" only.

(You can click on the link to https://www.pressreader.com/usa/the-washington-post/20070621/282664682972259 to read the story.)

QUESTIONS

[You are the spokesperson for the company. Pause and take a crack at answering each question *before* reading the feedback.]

> ➤ *If the rusty cans had gotten out into the public and been consumed by babies, and if those babies then became ill, what would Wyeth have done to compensate the families?*

{Feedback: Don't accept hypothetical questions. "I wouldn't want to guess what we'd do in a hypothetical situation. Instead, let me tell you about what we *are* doing for those impacted…"}

> ➤ *Does Wyeth often have trouble dealing with Philippine Bureau of Food and Drug red tape? Is it better to just go around them?*

{Feedback: Refute negative allegations without repeating them. Don't let the reporter put words in your mouth. And don't speak badly of the other side. "No. Next question" certainly makes it in under the 10-20 second mark.}

> ➤ *When did Wyeth know about the rusty cans? How long did it take to remove the cans from the shelves? How many cans total were recalled?*

{Feedback: Break down multiple part questions. Choose one question. Answer just that one. Move on to the next reporter without trying to remember all the other questions.}

> *What are the medical ramifications of an infant ingesting rust?*

{Feedback: Do not guess if it is outside your area of expertise. If you are not a doctor, nurse, or part of the medical profession, tell the reporter it's outside your area of expertise and you wouldn't want to hazard a guess.}

> *Would you say that the Philippine government blew the rust issue out of proportion because it is just trying to make it harder for large international companies to edge into the territory of local infant formula manufacturers?*

{Feedback: Never speak badly of the other side. And don't let a reporter put words in your mouth.}

> *Do you personally believe the recalled formula was safe for infant consumption?*

{Feedback: Do not guess if it is outside your area of expertise – your area of expertise in this case being your assigned role as spokesperson. It's a trick question because the reporter is counting on the company's answer being "yes" and your *personal* answer being "no." This may be a question you'll have to anticipate and answer in advance because it is at the crux of your ability to be spokesperson for the company. If your personal answer and the company's standpoint don't align, you may not be the right spokesperson for this issue. If you can't speak with conviction, your words are not likely to come across as sincere. Choose a different spokesperson or convince leadership the company needs to take a different tack rather than trying to justify the unjustifiable. Crisis management is often about doing the right thing rather than just trying to make the situation seem less wrong.}

9.1.13 Case Studies – Pizza Hut/Marriott and Hurricane Irma (2017)

People are your number one priority? Walk the walk. Saying one thing and demonstrating through actions that it's not true leaves stakeholders saying "shame on you."

As Hurricane Irma bore down on the Florida Keys in 2017, the mayors of local communities told Florida residents that now was the time to execute their evacuation plans, not to wait until roadways were jammed and gas supplies dwindled.

But Pizza Hut decided serving its customers trumped allowing minimum wage employees to get out of Jacksonville early. Employees who missed shifts to heed government warnings to get themselves and their families to safety, were written up and disciplined.[129]

Similarly, Marriott chartered a boat to evacuate Marriott resort guests stranded on St. Thomas when the airport closed following Hurricane Irma. But dozens of non-Marriott tourists were left with their jaws ajar when Marriott refused to save them too – despite hundreds of empty seats. The company claimed "liability" prevented them from finding a way to assist.[130]

Lesson learned: do the right thing. Don't make excuses for why you couldn't.

9.1.14 – Case Study Sago Mine (2010)

In 2016, former CEO of Massey Energy Don Blankenship was found guilty of conspiracy to willfully violate mine health and safety standards. He was sentenced to a year in prison and fined $250,000 for turning a blind eye to safety violations that led to an accident six years earlier which killed 29 miners.[131]

Lesson learned: why do the right thing? If not because it is the right thing to do, do it because senior execs are increasingly being held accountable.

9.2 Dos and Don'ts:

Don't:

- Embarrass or argue with a reporter.
- Demand that your remarks not be edited.
- Demand that an answer you've given not be used.
- State what you are about to say is "off the record" or not attributable to you[132]. If you've already said it, then it's on the record and you *will* look bad.

Reporters may attempt to push your buttons to get you to let down your guard – especially if they believe you are playing a role. Don't be drawn into a fight, not even to defend yourself or your organization against unfair allegations. It is very easy for a reporter to edit out their taunts and leave only your explosive rejoinder. After the words are out of your mouth, you can't ask for a "do over" or that your answers not be used. After is always too late to ask to go off the record. If your intention is to point the reporter in a direction for questioning to uncover information that bolsters what you have to say or if you are not an authorized spokesperson for your organization, consider whether off the record is really the best way to do this (unless your intention is to be a whistleblower).

Don't ask reporters if you can review their articles for accuracy. Of course you want to! But you've got to refrain. Doing so signals to the reporter that you don't trust their capability to get the story right. The best you can do is offer your business card at the end of the interview and, as sincerely as you can, explain that you know you went over a lot of technical material so if they want to double check anything you are available any time. (Make sure your cell phone number is on that card.)

Dos:

9.2.1 The Mic Is Always On

- If a reporter leaves a microphone in your face after you've answered the question, *stop*.

166

- The mic is always on – always – including during "testing."[133]

You may be winning the game. Sometimes the reporter isn't quite sure what their next move is, but they know they haven't quite gotten the full story or the quote they were hoping for. So they just wait. And wait. Silence is your friend. No one broadcasts silence. It won't be "dead air" during the broadcast. They'll just cut out the long pause during editing. They are counting on the fact that most people get uncomfortable with silence and will eventually fill that silence with the sound of their own voice. In other words, they'll elaborate if the mic is still there and the reporter is looking at them intently. Don't. Just wait it out. Eventually the reporter will move on to the next question. (Unless it's not a long pause after all because you went off script and dug yourself into the mud with your elaboration.)

If no next question comes, feel free to challenge with your wrap up. "Do you have any more questions? No? Thank you for your time." [More on this in the "winning the game" section of the next chapter – see section 10.4.]

Assume you are always on the record even when you seemingly have wrapped up the interview and the reporter is walking you to the door. Anything you say to a reporter is still on the record, even when they do not have a microphone in their hand.

And always assume the microphone is on, even during set up and testing.

When I was a journalist, I did a story on the development of the DC waterfront. At the time, the city was trying to take better advantage of prime space that hadn't been sufficiently developed, including a barge that had been tethered to the waterfront just shy of the 14th Street Bridge and which fishermen had used for 100 years to sell their wares. City folk knew the Maine Avenue pier was the place to go to get the freshest and cheapest seafood.

The city had put together a proposal to redevelop and gentrify the area, adding shops and restaurants. They mapped out what it would look like. Indeed, the new waterfront still had a spot for the fish stalls, but they were up on dry land, not the barge, and, as the fishermen explained, the rent was three times as expensive for small kiosks that were 1/3 the size of the former space. If forced into the new model, they claimed, their way of life would be decimated.

That was one side of the story. My next move was to get the city's perspective. I scheduled an interview with Assistant City Administrator Merrick Malone. As my camera operator set up for the interview, we chatted in Malone's office. He bragged about having a wardrobe full of so many suits he had a different one for *every day of the year*. His cocky and dismissive attitude made clear this was not a man who was in touch with those less fortunate, nor did he care about their concerns or have any intention of working with them to try to find a solution that worked for both sides.

Malone was slouched in his chair. The lighting was already set up. Paul, my camera operator, had already clipped a lavaliere microphone to Malone's tie. As is standard, I was seated with my back to Paul so that his camera lens would be positioned just over my shoulder, making the viewer at home feel like they were seated in the same room right next to the interviewer. Even though my eyes remained on Merrick Malone, I could hear Paul's movements still as he finished his preparations. And then I heard the very soft click that I knew meant he had begun recording. Without missing a beat nor indicating the interview had officially begun, I said, "the fishermen say they won't be able to afford to continue operating under your waterfront redevelopment model."

Malone responded, *"Oh they're so full of shit."*

Malone's PR person leapt up from the corner to say "Wait! That's not on record." But it was too late. I had the perfect encapsulation of the city's unfiltered, unguarded viewpoint on the matter.

You are *always* on record – even if the microphone does not appear to be on and even if there is no microphone in sight.

You can view a video clip of the Merrick Malone interview at https://www.rothstein.com/executing-crisis-supplemental-files/

9.2.2 Radio (or Phone) Interview Tips

- A live interview is very different from a taped interview.
- Watch out for "Uh," "Um," and "You know." [134]

For starters, you'll have more than 10-20 seconds to provide answers in interviews that are broadcast live, because there is no editing. But that doesn't mean that the most noteworthy snippet of what you say won't be edited into other stories later. Be deliberate with your answers. It's better to take a couple of seconds of pause to think before answering, rather than starting each answer with a buy-yourself-a-couple-of-seconds-of-time "filler" like an "um" or "uh."

Understand the parameters of the interview. It is fair to ask who else is being interviewed for the story and which journalist will be doing the interview. It's even fair to decline an interview and shut out a news organization if they're known for biased reporting. It is also fair to set the parameters of how much time you can spend on the interview.

If you have a pre-scripted statement or talking points and you are doing your press conference or interview via telephone, spread your papers out in front of you. Do not hold papers in your hands – it's a dead giveaway that you are reading because inevitably there will be some paper rustling. Reading just does not seem as sincere or genuine as the seemingly unscripted.

When I media-train spokespersons, I always make this point. Although most of what I trained Arkema to do during the time I was there stuck, this point did not. Listen to the second Rich Rowe press conference following the Crosby crisis. Not only did he not have his statement spread out on the table in front of him, he had the pages stapled together. Don't staple the pages together; the audience can hear the page turn!

You can listen to the audio clips illustrating the page turns at https://www.rothstein.com/executing-crisis-supplemental-files/

9.2.3 TV Interview Tips

- Drive out monotone. The more practice, the less fear and the greater the prospect that animation will reappear in the voice.

- Look at the reporter, not the camera.
- Do an earphone check. Ask what to do if it pops out of your ear.[135]
- Don't swivel in your chair.[136]

9.2.3.1 Don't Memorize

Practice but don't memorize your talking points. The more you become familiar with the material and the points you are trying to make, the better chance you'll be able to say it conversationally.

If you memorize your talking points you run the risk of sounding robotic. When his 2016 presidential campaign was foundering, Florida Senator Marco Rubio began to repeat the same talking point again and again during a debate and made himself the brunt of jokes on late night television.

Fig. 9-1 Memorizing can make you sound robotic. See
https://www.vox.com/2016/2/6/10929738/marco-rubio-debate

9.2.3.2 Look the Reporter in the Eye

Conversation is key. The reporter is not your adversary and he or she may actually become less adversarial the more sincere your answers really are. Think about the stakeholders you are actually trying to reach.

How would you explain what was happening to them? Speak to the reporter as if you are talking to your true audience. Think of the reporter as proxy for them. Look the reporter in the eye. If you instead turn to the camera and speak to the camera, it's not only a sign of disrespect to the reporter but also comes off as less sincere, as if you are just using them instead of having a conversation with them.

There are two exceptions:

1. If the reporter is being adversarial and it is a live interview, ignore the adversarial question and turn instead directly to the camera when you say "I want to speak to the public directly when I say…" This is very difficult to carry off, so do this with extreme caution.
2. If there is no reporter present and you are doing a live interview with a TV anchor who is in their studio in another location. In that case, the only way to seemingly look the interviewer in the eye is to look directly into the camera lens.

A word of caution on this: When reporters do their "stand-ups" – that is, when they wrap up their story on camera live from the location of the event – the camera person will often set up a monitor right next to the camera that projects a picture of how they have framed the shot, so the reporter can see what they look like on air. But they are professionals and as soon as the shot goes live they know to turn their eyes to the camera instead of the monitor of themselves. When a camera person is sent to interviews without a reporter, they still may set up a monitor to show you what the shot looks like. I've found that with non-TV journalists, there is a tendency to keep looking at themselves in that monitor during the interview. Don't look at yourself on the TV monitor once the interview has begun – it just looks weird!

Similarly, with Skype interviews, be sure you look at the camera lens. This Skype reporter is reading off her screen slightly below the camera and because her eyes are on the monitor instead of looking into the lens, it doesn't feel as if she's looking us in the eye:

171

Fig. 9-2. Look them in the eye at https://www.youtube.com/watch?v=lc3UZ0lWNng

Don't swivel in your chair. If you are given a chair that swivels, ask instead for a standard chair (or ask to stand up for the interview). You will be nervous. Everyone is. Swivel chairs exacerbate the situation by making it too easy for your nervous energy to manifest in constant side-to-side swiveling. It can become fascinatingly distracting in about 10 seconds – but not in a good way. Instead of listening to what you have to say, the audience will be captivated by how nervous you are.

9.2.4 Quiz

We'll use the "University Accused of Lying to Hide Killing" story from earlier in this chapter to give the following quiz questions a little context.[137]

> *A reporter calls to say they'd like to set up a phone interview with the university spokesperson regarding Eastern Michigan University's side of the Laura Dickinson murder investigation. What are your "rights?" What should you ask in the process of setting up this interview?*

{Feedback: Who will be doing the interview? How much time are you looking for? Who else are you interviewing for this story?}

> *Is it appropriate to offer your email address to the reporter at the end of the interview, asking whether they'll send you an advance*

172

copy of the story, just to double check that they got the technical details about the DNA evidence right?

{Feedback: Absolutely offer your email address and cell phone number to the reporter so that they can feel free to reach out if they have any additional questions or need clarification on anything you talked about. Do not indicate what you think of their mental acuity. It is not okay to ask for an advance copy of the story. They're not going to let you review the story to make sure they got it right and the request is going to appear adversarial.}

> ➤ *If the reporter is painting the university in a bad light, is it okay to "stick up for" the university and put the reporter "in his place?"*

{Feedback: Don't pick fights with reporters. You'll look like a hothead. They'll cut out their adversarial questions in the finished on-air story and you will be the only one shouting.}

> ➤ *Every time I give an interview to that reporter he seems to twist my words around and make the story more sensational than it should be. Can I request that he not be assigned to this story?*

{Feedback: No. But you can decline the interview, and probably should. Just make sure you accept all other interviews with all other journalists. The exclusion will send a message to the station.}

> ➤ *If the person calling to set up the interview indicates this is going to be a short interview to be used as part of a news package, can I ask that the interview be shown in its entirety – so as to eliminate my words being taken out of context?*

{Feedback: No. The onus is on you to make sure that every answer out of your mouth is a self-contained gem that lasts no longer than 10-20 seconds, so that it won't matter which answer the reporter chooses. They won't need to edit your answer and you minimize the possibility your answer will be taken out of context.}

> ➤ *Can I point out that the national advocacy group Security on Campus has been making inflammatory and not always accurate*

*statements… and ask that they not be interviewed as part of the
same story in which my interview will appear?*

{Feedback: You don't have the right to make demands about who else
the journalist chooses to balance the story. But you do have the right to
decline the interview, with explanation.}

> *If I flub an answer, is it okay to ask for a "do-over"?*

{Feedback: There are no do-overs.}

> *If I am willing to point the reporter in the right direction to get
> the right answers, but don't want to be interviewed on camera
> because of the sensitive nature of the investigation, what are the
> ground rules that have to be set?*

{Feedback: Off the record and not for attribution (you'll do the interview
but don't want your name used) ground rules need to be set in advance.
Once the information is out of your mouth, it can't be taken back.}

9.3 What Not to Wear on TV

Men:

- Avoid patterned suits, stripes, checks.
- Sit on your coattails – it pulls your jacket down so it fits snugly
  on your shoulders and makes your jacket hang better.
- Use makeup if offered, especially bald men. Bright studio lights
  bouncing off a bald shiny head can be overly distracting.

Women:

- Avoid distracting jewelry and any accessories that jangle.
- Wear everyday makeup in neutral shades.
- Wear makeup even if you never wear makeup[138].

Cameras can sometimes have difficulty with herringbone patterns,
narrow pinstripes, or any tiny pattern with starkly different colors. That's
because the lens doesn't know which color to focus on so shifts back and
forth between the colors causing jittering. It's very distracting and the last
thing you want is for the audience to be distracted from the message you

are trying to convey. Borrow a colleague's tie or remove the offending tie completely and unbutton the first button of your shirt. If it's your shirt that's the offender, don a jacket. I coach execs to consider keeping a camera-ready option always at the ready hanging on the back of their door.

Here's a clip demonstrating pinstripe shirt jitter:

Fig. 9-3 Pinstripe shirt jitter at https://www.youtube.com/watch?v=jXEgnRWRJfg

Depending on the emergency or crisis, (and assuming you've got a solid colored shirt) even executives may want to consider doffing the jacket entirely and rolling up their sleeves. It sends a message that they are in the midst of working on a solution rather than hanging out at corporate headquarters. Keep in mind, this usually only works if you are on scene rather than still at corporate headquarters.

As William Hurt coached Albert Brooks in the 1987 movie "Broadcast News", if you are doing a studio interview and wearing a suit jacket, sit on the coat tails if they are long enough. This will pin the shoulders down and create a nice clean line.

Fig. 9-4. Sit on your coat tails at https://vimeo.com/67010349

If your skin is very dark, avoid wearing white for camera interviews, especially in bright sunlight. That's because cameras adjust their exposure on the fly, and the reflection from white may cause the areas of the frame that are not white to look much darker. Your features very well could be wiped out unless the photographer is carefully adjusting for your skin tone.

Fig. 9-5. People with dark skin tones may want to be careful wearing white unless the photographer can adjust for skin tone. See guidance from Elena Wilkins at https://digital-photography-school.com/how-to-photograph-mixed-skin-tones/

Fig. 9.6. More guidance on exposing for darker skin tones at https://jezebel.com/the-truth-about-photography-and-brown-skin-1557656792

It is okay to wear a company logo, but remove ball caps, jackets, etc. with advertising for someone else's company.

If your skin is shiny under the lights, ask for powder. Bald men may need powder for the top of their head, because the glare of the lights can be distracting. The tipoff will be if the camera person asks whether you'd like a little powder? Always say yes. Similarly, women who are natural beauties should wear a little makeup anyway. TV lights really are unforgiving.

As with swivel chairs and glaring bald heads, minimize chunky jewelry that could distract from what you have to say, especially if you are wearing a lavaliere mic pinned to your lapel and the necklace bumps into the mic every time you turn your head.

If you wear glasses but can take them off without squinting, take them off. Consider nonglare glasses if you are a frequent spokesperson and must wear glasses. Never wear sunglasses or transition glasses outdoors. People want to see your eyes. Most people feel they can tell whether you are telling the truth in your eyes.

This was a point I always make when doing media training. Arkema spokesman Rich Rennard remembered to take his glasses off as a result when he did his press conference at Crosby. Putting the glasses on top of his head wasn't the best choice, but the most important thing was that viewers could see his eyes.

Fig. 9-7. Viewers want to see your eyes https://www.youtube.com/watch?v=zs5cExp-OFA

Summary

Media training is best done face-to-face to gain from feedback, and because you are likely not to recognize your own quirky or distracting mannerisms. This chapter covered pitfalls for spokespersons, dos and don'ts, and what not to wear for interviews. But don't try this at home; practice this advice as a team.

Questions for Further Thought and Discussion

➤ *Describe a time when you fell into one of the reporter traps identified in this chapter. What could you have done differently which might have led to a better outcome?*

➤ *Think about a time when your organization was in a crisis. How can you answer the following question without allowing the reporter to put words in your mouth, without using jargon, and without going over three sentences (20 seconds) of explanation: "What happened and why did you hide the truth for so long?"*

➤ *At the beginning of this chapter, there was a caution about possible blind spots when reading through media training techniques instead of practicing them live. Using one of the exercises above, ask a colleague to quiz you with the questions, and to provide feedback on your answers (with particular focus on distracting body language quirks you may be unaware of).*

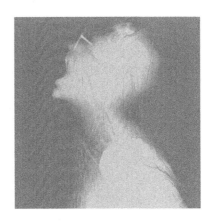

CHAPTER 10

COMMUNICATIONS STRATEGY

We know that it is necessary to immediately begin communicating in a crisis [see sections 1.4 and 2.1.1], especially since if we, the most informed source, don't, others will.

For 38 excruciating minutes in January 2018, everyone who had a cell phone in Hawaii scrambled for cover and told their loved ones goodbye – because they believed that missiles were incoming.

"Ballistic missile threat inbound to Hawaii. This is not a drill" read the 8:07 A.M. text from the state's emergency management agency.

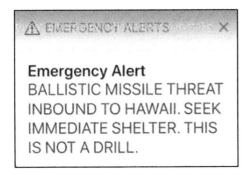

It was a false alarm, a mistake made by a state employee who had erroneously pushed the wrong button. But it wasn't the mistake that angered Hawaiians. It was the inexplicable delay getting the correction out.[139]

In January 2013, chemical manufacturer Lubrizol accidentally released mercaptan, the chemical added to odorless natural gas to make it stink, from its Rouen France factory. Though not toxic, the foul odor, "like a giant French fart," could be smelled for hundreds of miles from Paris to Britain's shores and prompted emergency calls from residents.

Lubrizol did not use its social media tools to communicate what was happening. But others did – including emergency responders who stepped into the void with competency and humor to answer questions and reassure the public.

Police in the coastal English town of Hastings reassured residents with #Noneedtopanic tweets.[140]

The London Fire Brigade received five times more calls about potential gas leaks before 10:30 A.M. than they took all of the day before. Their response #mondieu[141].

Ben Boobier
@bboobier

Why does the whole of Hastings smell of oil?

ColinM
@m1tchc

A very odd oily smell over Hastings this morning. Anyone else noticed it?

Metropolitan Police
@metpoliceuk

We are aware of reports of a strong noxious gas like smell in some South East London boroughs – no risk to public

---

Hastings Police
@Hastings_police

The smell in the air today in Hastings is Mercaptan it is a non toxic gas and has originated from Rouen #noneedtopanic

---

LeanneSS
@LeanneS1971

@Hastings_police We've all been searching our houses today! Can't believe that stink isn't toxic – made me feel sick! Bleurgggghhh

---

Hastings Police
@Hastings_police

@LeanneS1971 put some Vicks on a tissue or carry a scented pomander, might help

Unlike Lubrizol, school officials in Atlanta used Twitter that same month to let parents know about a shooting, including that the injured student had been transported to the hospital, that schools were on lockdown, what time parents could pick up their kids and the procedure for doing so, that police had taken the suspect into custody, all in real time.[142]

ATL Public Schools @apsupdate
An Atlanta Public Schools student has suffered a gunshot injury at Price Middle School.
4:20 PM – 31 Jan 13

ATL Public Schools @apsupdate
The injured student has been transported to Grady Hospital. Suspect in custody.
4:21 PM – 31 Jan 13

ATL Public Schools @apsupdate
Update: we are releasing Price walking students first at normal dismissal time.
4:32 PM – 31 Jan 13

ATL Public Schools @apsupdate
Carpool riders at Price will be released second, followed by buses.
4:33 PM – 31 Jan 13

- *Determining in advance what information your key stakeholders will need and how to get it into their hands quickly.*
- *Logistics for small organizations with limited communications staff.*
- *The role of the crisis wingman.*
- *How to win the game.*
- *Effective messaging and bridging techniques.*
- *Communication strategies with victims.*
- *Employees as spokespersons.*
- *Shaping the narrative.*

10.1 Actionable Information

What actionable information might *your* organization need to get out in real time in a crisis? How can you use your organization's social media tools to do so (rather than letting others step into the void to communicate for you)?

Key stakeholders, especially community members most impacted, will search for information using web and social media sources, and can be quite irritated if you aren't keeping up.

As SimpliFlying notes in its 2013 slideshare, Asiana Airlines missed the boat multiple times in its failure to use social media tools effectively following the crash landing of flight OZ214 at San Francisco airport.[143]

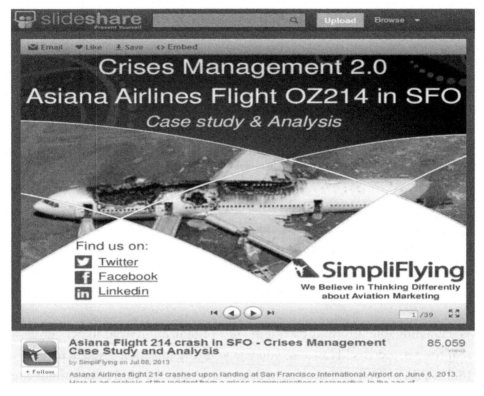

Fig. 10-1. SimpliFlying slideshare at https://www.slideshare.net/shanxz/asiana-flight-214-crash-in-sfo-crises-management-case-study-and-analysis

According to the timeline, although the first photo of the crash was posted on social media thirty seconds after the crash, it took Asiana Airlines more than four hours before it released its first statement and sent its first Tweet.

Airline manufacturers and other airlines used social media to issue condolences to the families. And the National Transportation Safety Board used social media to provide regular updates, as well as photos from the scene.

Although it was the middle of the night for Asiana Airlines, the public wasn't forgiving about the lack of comment.

As this infographic from the slideshare shows, people *want* to get their information directly from the source and will seek out the company's channels.

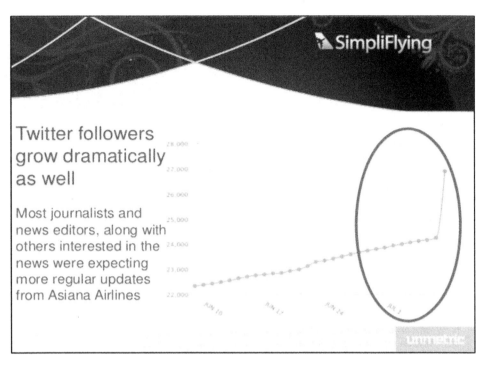

Fig. 10-2. SimpliFlying analysis indicates the public flocked to Asiana's social media sites to try to get their information from the company itself. https://www.slideshare.net/shanxz/asiana-flight-214-crash-in-sfo-crises-management-case-study-and-analysis

Not taking advantage of the ability to speak directly (and unfiltered) to stakeholders allowed other lesser-informed sources to step up to the mic and spread rumors and misunderstanding.

The accidental spokesperson may not always be right

While Krista Seiden happened to be at the right place at he right time, not all her information was accurate. For example, the flight did not arrive from Taipei.

Soon after, some journalists mis-interpreted that 60 un-accounted for passengers were actually fatalities.

If Asiana was participating online, it could have corrected these facts.

Krista Seiden @kristaseiden   7 Jul
Hearing reports the #planecrash at #SFO is an Asiana 777 in from Taipei. Lots of emergency respondents onsite pic.twitter.com/6FNXRcHm1o

Fig. 10-3. SimpliFlying example of inaccurate reporting by an eyewitness whose erroneous account was picked up by the media because the company didn't step forward with accurate information quickly. https://www.slideshare.net/shanxz/asiana-flight-214-crash-in-sfo-crises-management-case-study-and-analysis

10.2 Logistics for Smaller Organizations with Limited Communications Staff

Quick, impactful communication with a wide reach need not be confined to organizations with deep resources; it just takes some thought and planning. Just because an organization has resources, doesn't mean they've thought through every detail, and that is often the difference between messages that resonate with the audiences they were intended to reach, rather than bungled because no one thought through the details sufficiently.

Case in point: In this 1991 welcoming ceremony with (6'2") then-President George H. W. Bush and Queen Elizabeth (5'4"), the Queen's message was all but lost because White House staff neglected to pull out a stepstool for her use, nor lower the lectern to an appropriate height. The resulting image of a "talking hat" was so amusing that few paid any attention to what she had to say.

Fig. 10-4 The talking hat can be found at https://www.youtube.com/watch?v=p-8pz7Ot-WI

Pay attention to what's in the background as well. Conservative Attorney General John Ashcroft (who served in the George W. Bush administration from 2001-2005) did not cotton well to the juxtaposition of the bare-breasted Spirit of Justice statue behind his head. Curtains were installed to block the statue from view for the rest of his tenure.[144]

Fig. 10-5. More on the Spirit of Justice statue at the State Department can be found at http://www.kamenko.com/news/politics/washington-politics/ashcroft-addresses-employees-at-the-justice-department https://www.cbsnews.com/news/cover-up-at-justice-department

Rather than allow others to speak for you and to frame the story, take control of the elements you control. This is an important distinction. The media certainly control which of your soundbites they choose to use. We've already discussed your every answer being a self-contained gem [see section 9.1.4] so that it doesn't matter which answer the media choose and you won't be taken out of context. But what else do you control and how can you take back control of certain elements by presenting them yourself instead of allowing the media (and others) to filter what you say?

It's acceptable to record and post video clips of your spokesperson's comments. In fact, it is essential. It furthers your ability to take control of the elements you can control in framing the story and how it is portrayed.

Even very small organizations can play in this sandbox.

Choose a background that is interesting or colorful or in context rather than just a boring (often this screams amateurish) blank white wall. But beware your background doesn't become *too* visually interesting and take away from what you have to say.

Here's an example of too visually interesting:

Fig. 10-6. Too visually interesting at *https://www.youtube.com/watch?v=Z41A3p-L0fE*

It is possible to use a mobile device rather than a video camera and microphone. But if you must use one, ensure the device is no more than a couple of feet away from the subject so the built-in microphone's audio pick up will be as clear as possible.

Use a tripod or other stabilizer rather than handholding the recording device. Even a selfie-stick is better than nothing.

If doing a Skyped interview or video recording, take a few minutes to prepare a more well-composed shot.

Don't look down on a laptop. Everyone knows that when you take a selfie you've got to hold your phone up high; the same goes here. Boost your laptop up on a couple of sturdy books so the built-in camera lens is at least at face level rather than looking up your nose. Put a couple of lights to the side; nothing fancy necessary. Softer lightbulbs are better than harsh lighting.

Here are a few minimal techniques for better lighting without a lot of effort:

Fig. 10-7. Minimal techniques for better lighting can be found at
https://www.youtube.com/watch?v=Tin5q2-yPew&list=PLB938E50055C56A51

Fig. 10-8. Minimal techniques for better lighting can be found at
https://www.youtube.com/watch?v=d5uybmobdFY
https://www.youtube.com/watch?v=v0FWNXEDzDE

Fig. 10-9. Minimal techniques for better lighting can be found at
https://www.youtube.com/watch?v=FINpcXNo5iU

Aim for a statement that is a minute or less. The point of trying to keep your recorded statement short is because without the use of a teleprompter, your spokesperson is less likely to be able to genuinely and sincerely convey the organization's messages without memorizing (which usually comes across as stilted) or reading them. DO NOT READ A STATEMENT – that just screams insincerity and pre-scripting.

Review the Brown's Bar example in the chapter on apology. [See section 8.9.] Does the owner's statement, read from a script, in any way appear sincere? He'd have been much better off jotting down his talking points in bullet form, reviewing them until he was familiar with them… then speaking conversationally to the camera. Even if it took a couple of takes and even if the statement wasn't word for word, its impact would have been more genuine. This apology was less than worthless, it was counterproductive.

Fig. 10-10. Reading from a script does not look sincere – see http://vimeo.com/44816688

Blue Bell's CEO Paul Kruze provides an example of a video clip done simply and fairly effectively. The background was interesting but not too interesting. Lighting was fine, but not perfect; he could have used a bit more lighting on his face. Though he probably had a teleprompter, the statement wasn't too long and hit the key points. Additional information accompanied the statement on the company's website.[145]

Fig. 10-11. Blue Bell video clip done simply at
https://www.youtube.com/watch?v=yphTqJmVD1A

Video clips do not necessarily need to include a spokesperson. One of the earliest and most well-known examples of crisis communications done well is a video news release issued by Pepsi in the 1993 syringe case.

During the 1993 alleged tampering incident, Pepsi refused to recall their products, releasing video news releases that showed the perpetrator caught on surveillance video inserting a needle into a can of Pepsi,[146] as well as another video clip of the production line which demonstrated how quickly the line was moving and left viewers with a better understanding of how impossible it would have been for a syringe to have been inserted during the bottling process. It was effective because rather than Pepsi *telling* customers "trust us, it's impossible," viewers came to the conclusion on their own.

Fig. 10-12. Pepsi bottling process video clip demonstrated beyond all reasonable doubt that a syringe could not have been inserted during the bottling process at https://www.youtube.com/watch?v=wi9xDEIHuWA

10.3 The Crisis Wingman

In addition to background visuals, carefully consider the logistics of the introduction and graceful exit from a press conference situation. A "wingman" (or -woman) can be invaluable here. This wingman should not actually be a spokesperson but clearly an aide whose responsibility is paving the way for their boss. This allows them to fly under the radar without being expected to answer questions.

The wingman should be the person who identifies where the spokesperson will hold the press conference and where they will stand. When holding a press conference (or interview) outdoors on scene, consider lighting basics and opt for a spot where bright sunlight doesn't cause harsh, unflattering shadows. Media photographers are pretty good at quickly framing an interesting background if given an extra minute, but don't leave this completely up to the media because they will certainly identify an interesting background that may not always be in the spokesperson's best interests: the ruins of a factory fire may not make the best backdrop from the company's perspective. The wingman should scout the location in advance and when pressured into putting the spokesperson in the location suggested by the media, needs to stand firm. (The wingman and spokesperson must coordinate in advance on where and why as to the best location.)

In the following example, you can see this did not happen. The media captured the spokesperson in an awkward location with no means to gracefully exit. When the spokesperson decided the press conference was over, the media could have blocked the exit, making it difficult to leave. Especially when holding a press conference indoors, ensure there is nothing between the lectern and the door. Nothing.

Here's an example of a spokesperson surrounded on all sides by journalists, leaving no good exit path if the questioning turned ugly:

Fig. 10-13. Example of a spokesperson with no avenue for escape at
https://www.youtube.com/watch?v=WVRhn7Nja5g

Here's another example of a badly placed location for the spokesperson. In this case, when LeBron James had his fill of a reporter's questioning and decided to end the press conference, he had to make his way from the front corner of the room through a sea of reporters and cameras in order to exit through the door at the very back of the room. He was lucky that the reporters were courteous enough not to stop his walkout. In many circumstances, reporters are not always so polite:

Fig. 10-14. Try not to talk yourself into a corner at
https://www.youtube.com/watch?v=Tk_EBNLyqxw

Always start a press conference when you've announced you will hold the press conference. If you've said the press conference will begin at 2 P.M., begin the press conference at 2 P.M. The media will have scheduled their news coverage around cutting to the news conference at the stated time and if you don't begin on time, it will force the on-scene reporter to vamp with what they know (or rumors that are circulating), and they'll interview "eyewitnesses" or "authorities" (or each other) to fill time until the official spokesperson finally appears. All of this additional chit chat just exacerbates the misinformation problem.

As the media arrive on location leading up to the start of the press conference, the wingman can be available to assist them in pointing out where the spokesperson will be standing, where microphones can be placed, exactly when the spokesperson will arrive… While making clear that he/she is not involved in anything but the logistics of this press conference (and certainly not in the crisis decision-making or latest on the situation), the wingman should set any parameters or expectations such as how long the spokesperson has available, whether they will have a short update or statement before taking questions, how much time the spokesperson has to take questions, name and title of the spokesperson... The wingman should ensure any background information or facility stats and the spokesperson's bio is available in advance (to help the media prep intelligent, on-topic questions and ensure the spokesperson's name is spelled right in the Chyron identifier superimposed on the television screen).

A good wingman will also read the situation and be prepared to step in to end the press conference.

Press conferences should end roughly when scheduled to. Not too soon or it will appear the organization is only interested in conveying the information it wants to convey rather than being up front with answers to questions the journalists are interested in getting answers to. The spokesperson should remain and answer questions until the questions have been answered. The wingman should read the room and make a determination when the game has been won (more on this in a moment.) Once the questions become repetitive because the reporters no longer can think of additional questions but haven't yet won the game is the time for the wingman to step up to announce the spokesperson has time for one more question.

The wingman should also be vigilant to ensure the spokesperson is not digging themselves into a hole without realizing they're foundering and far afield of the messages they're trying to convey. This may happen on occasion if the media land an unanticipated question and the spokesperson can't figure out how to bridge back to their messages. Once they've started down this path, it may become like a feeding frenzy and the spokesperson may get further and further underwater. If this happens, the wingman must be prepared to step in to indicate time is up. ("_____ has time for one more question.")

Anthony Weiner's press conference following his admission of sexting is a good example of what it looks like when a spokesperson, absent a wingman stepping in to say "one more question," doesn't extricate himself when he's got nothing left to gain by remaining. In this case, Weiner had already repeated his messages a *dozen* times, though the media kept at it. Rather than recognize that all the questions were circular and that he was just digging himself in deeper and deeper, he remained and continued answering questions that advanced nowhere.

Fig. 10-15. Spokesperson absent a wingman to recognize when the messages had been delivered and there was nothing left to gain at http://www.youtube.com/watch?v=mjsE4AZZgbc

It is probably best not to have the spokesperson act as their own wingman, not only because it is difficult for the spokesperson to objectively realize they are going down in flames, but because, as the official spokesperson, they cannot realistically set ground rules or parameters.

Gary Southern [see section 2.3.1] fell into this trap when he attempted to end the Freedom Industries press conference after just a couple of minutes once he recognized he was abysmally unprepared. Just as bad, once he made the decision to ditch, he allowed himself to be dragged right back into the fray of continuing to answer questions. A wingman could have told him to stop talking and dragged him off by the elbow.

A spokesperson also cannot adequately act as their own wingman when it comes to setting parameters for the press conference. Chief Charles Moose infamously attempted to set the ground rules for the first press conference during the DC sniper crisis in which two gunmen terrorized the metropolitan Washington, D.C. area in October 2002 with 10 sniper killings and three critical injuries, executed from their Chevrolet Caprice sedan. Just before the press conference was set to begin, Moose stepped to the mics to let the press know the official press conference would begin shortly but first he wanted to ensure they understood the ground rules.

"You are going to follow these rules… Don't make me look like an ass."

- Chief Charles Moose, during the DC sniper shootings

While Moose thought his briefing of the ground rules was understood to be off the record, the media had a field day with the video clip and paternalistic tone he took. Essentially, they allowed him to make himself look like what he didn't want to look like.

Don't tell the media how to do their job. And never assume anything is off the record once the spokesperson has stepped into the room. Once the spokesperson is present, the press conference (or interview) has begun.

10.4 Winning the Game

Always keep in mind that doing an interview or holding a press conference is like engaging in a sports match. The media are not necessarily your adversaries, but they aren't necessarily on your side either. Traditionally, they're not supposed to be on anyone's side; they're supposed to be doing their best to report both sides. Often, they really will narrow it down to just two sides in black and white without a lot of nuanced color in between. However, an organization in crisis is often not the underdog, especially if there have been victims or damages, so you won't necessarily be starting from a level playing field and will have to convince harder to win.

When it comes to "winning," that's both your and the media's objective, but how to get there differs.

For the media, they want to get a good story that is interesting to their audience and which fairly and accurately portrays the facts. (If they can't get that, but you say something stupid, that can be just as interesting.) When it comes to crisis, that sometimes means exposing a wrong and calling the bad guy on the carpet for his mistakes. More often than not, if your organization has made a mistake and it's in crisis, it's going to be portrayed as the bad guy.

For the organization in crisis, winning the game means turning the tide from being the bad guy to being able to change the public's opinion of you, what happened, and what you are doing to fix the wrong.

Prepare for crisis now. I will repeat it: crisis communication never begins on the day of the crisis. Identify your spokespersons. Yes, plural. Ensure they've been media-trained and the team is on the same page with regard to strategy. (More on employees as spokespersons in a moment.) Ensure there is a process and structure in place to begin communicating as quickly as possible.

Identify and vet what can be said. Ensure those who are authorized to speak on behalf of the organization know the parameters of what they can talk about. Ensure they know what things they can always talk about or what the organization's hip pocket statements are. [See section 1.3.]

Having these things in place in advance will give you the ability to take advantage of the grace period between when a situation occurs and when the situation becomes known and you need to begin communicating. Spend those few minutes working with your team of trusted advisors to anticipate questions and develop answers. Go beyond what, when, where to also anticipate the questions you hope don't get asked about why and how.

- Anticipate likely questions and think through responses.
- Answer media inquiries as quickly as possible. Be courteous and helpful to reporters.
- Don't say "no comment."
- Stick to the facts – don't speculate.
- Disclose key facts all at once – even if the news is bad.
- Ensure families have been notified before releasing information on victims.
- Monitor media coverage so you can correct any serious errors quickly.

I used to work with Pete McCarthy, a wise media trainer and public relations professional, who coached: "Whoever frames the issue wins. Everyone else plays catch up."

In other words, if you (the organization) delay in setting the stage of what happened, you'll be backed into a defensive, rather than offensive, posture. Even if you did nothing wrong, the negative publicity can be damaging and you may never right your reputation in the minds of those who only ever got the other side's viewpoint before you finally joined the game and started responding.

For example, a truck driver delivering a load of material to a chemical facility in the summer of 2015 misunderstood the plant's strict "no idle" policy (a safety measure to minimize the chance of setting off an explosion) while loading or unloading. Truck drivers are not only required to shut off their engines, they are also required to remain within 25' of their vehicles. Rather than park the truck and sit it out in the air-conditioned break room with a large window overlooking the unloading area, the truck driver sat it out in the cab of his truck with the windows closed and the temperature soaring to 140 degrees.

Company staff noticed the truck driver slumped over the steering wheel of his truck and called emergency services. An ambulance transported the truck driver to the hospital.

But that's just the beginning of the story.

The truck driver posted this selfie on the popular trucking magazine's CDLife.com site along with his framing of the story. In his version of the story, the trucker claimed he thought he was not allowed to be in the air-conditioned break room.[147]

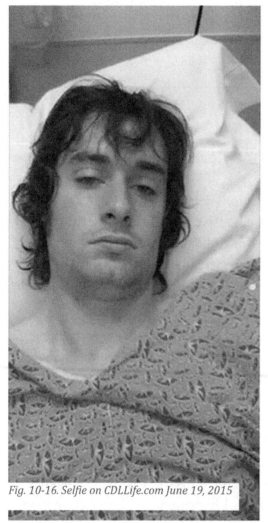

Fig. 10-16. Selfie on CDLLife.com June 19, 2015

The CDLife.com site exploded with more than 1,400 comments before social media monitoring picked up on the brewing crisis and the company had a chance to add its two cents. By that time, no amount of apology or explanation was going to undo the perception fellow truck drivers had about what had happened… even though the truck driver backed down from his story immediately and refused to be quoted by name in a follow up story on "How to stay safe when the heat's got you beat" in the aligned Land Line magazine for truckers a few weeks later.[148]

CDLLife.com
June 19, 2015
DRIVER TIP:
"The dangers of a heat stroke. This was me yesterday. I was at the customer in Courtland, VA. It was 98 degrees outside and well over 100 degrees inside the truck… the customer has a strict no idle policy. They also do not allow drivers in any of their break rooms or have a drivers lounge. I spoke with the loader and she said to remain inside the truck during the entire process. So no idle, no break room, no drivers lounge, and must remain inside the truck during the entire

Shay Shay Kenney I guess none of you have ever delt [sic] with a hazmat situation were [sic] any heat spark or flame could cause a major explosion your not sitting with the doors open against a dock and lot times yiu [sic] also have to wear special clothing which is also hot and uncomfortable…

Brett Cook You will sweat your ass off wearing frc [fire retardant] clothing in the summer sitting in a truck that is shut off. Some places will allow you to use your apu, [sic] some won't.

George Stedman I am a driver and if its hot in the truck its runnin [sic] until someone comes and trys [sic] to take the keys!

> **Adam Winters** Sometimes rules do not apply and if they said no loading while idled then call dispatch…

> We are very sorry that this driver suffered heat stroke and we are investigating the circumstances. For safety reasons… requires that drivers remain within 25' of their vehicles and not idle their trucks near flammable materials. However, there was an air conditioned room within range and we are trying to determine why the driver did not remain in that room.

10.5 Messaging

Messages, simply put, are your organization's side of the story, framed positively in terms of the actions you are taking to make the situation right, whether you are at fault or not. That is not the same as creating positive spin, especially if that spin is artificial wordsmithing bent on making a situation *seem* less bad than it really is. Messages go beyond objective truth about the facts to position your organization's truth and counter the negative positioning that may be cast on you by rumors, outrage from perceived injustice, or even the fact that your organization has some right-making to do as a result of what just happened.

When beginning an interview or press conference, introduce yourself unless this has already been done. Simplify your title. Your exact title isn't necessary, instead, the reporter needs to know the context of why you are speaking on behalf of the organization. Your title can be as simple as "[Organization] Spokesperson," unless you are giving a particular point of view ("CEO, [Organization]" or "Engineering Manager, [Organization]." Expect to start with a situation status update briefly explaining the what, where, when, or what is latest. If victims are involved, offer regret, apology, humanization.

- In advance, think through the two or three main points you want to make.
- Start the interview by identifying yourself and the latest information on the incident.
- Begin bridging to your key messages.

By this point your messages should be in full swing. Put the situation in context. Explain what you are doing to make the situation right. Focus on what is important. Get across your messages to those you are trying to reach on the other side of the media. Then, and only then, ask what questions the media has.

If the media jump the gun and barrage you with questions from the start, calmly hold up your hand and explain you'd like to start with some information and *then* you'll be happy to take their questions. You may be able to head off many of their questions by starting this way. Once the questioning begins, always try to find a way to bridge back to your key messages.

If you are noticing that you have circled back to each of your message points twice, you have won your game. Stop playing! You have nothing left to gain from continuing to field questions. Of course the media will continue to try to engage you because *they* have not won by backing you into a corner where they flummox you and wheedle an off-script answer, so they will continue to try to ask questions. But if you stop after you have delivered your messages (in 20 second or less soundbites), they will have to choose the soundbite that summarizes your organization's point of view from amongst the answers you have given – your messages – or the points you intended to make all along.

10.6 Bridging

Bridging is a transition from where you don't want to be with the conversation... to where you do want to be.

Always answer the question asked. Not answering appears manipulative. You may not be able to answer negative questions with a positive response, so keep it short and then bridge to one of your messages/talking points.

Transitional phrases may include:

> *... but what is important to keep in mind is...*

> *... but what we are currently doing to help is...*

For example:

Reporter question: *"How many people are without a home tonight as a result of the evacuation?"*

Your answer: *"Approximately a dozen families were impacted, **but what is important to keep in mind is** that we are doing our best to take care of all their needs. We have housed each family in a local hotel and have provided vouchers for meals and transportation for the next several days."*

The passive voice is effective in this kind of communication. It enables the speaker to say "mistakes were made" rather than "we made mistakes." (This is especially valuable when it is not clear whether your organization is at fault.) But it can be seen as evading responsibility if your organization clearly is to blame. The above example is an effective transition from "stuff happened" to "here is what we are doing about it" with a definite, active voice phrase. We are doing our best to take care of all of their needs, regardless of who is to blame.

Reporter question: *"What if the community incident rate of cancer increases in 10 years as a result of the toxic release?"*

Your answer: *"I don't know what the long-term impacts will be and would not want to speculate, **but what we are currently doing to help is** to ensure each and every person affected receives a full medical checkup on our dime by their own trusted physician or care provider. We will pick up the cost of any medical treatment recommended by their care provider, whether or not the incident is deemed to be our fault."*

10.7 Communications Strategy with Victims

Communications strategy with people who have been impacted negatively by your organization's event needs to focus on *their* needs. First, identify who has been affected. Second, identify what they need in order to put this behind them. What can you say to encourage this closure? Ensure your messages to affected parties are full of action verbs about what you are *doing*, not trying to do or hoping to do.

Media trainer and public relations professional Pete McCarthy sums it up this way:

- Identify the affected parties.
- Develop message points that will encourage closure,
- Use action verbs to carry your message.

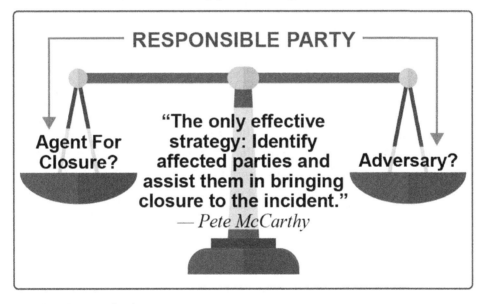

Fig. 10-17. Strategy for closure.

10.8 Employees as Spokespersons

In my experience, most organizations identify authorized spokespersons and write a media policy stipulating that no one else may speak to the media on behalf of the company. But is that truly best practice? [See chapter 5.]

In one organization where I worked, we determined the better – albeit unusual – choice was to authorize *all* employees to speak to the media. Our reasoning was that in an emergency situation, they'd be sought out by the media and we really had no realistic way to stop them from talking anonymously or covertly (and especially on social media). We knew what they had to say was already going to be highly esteemed within their own circles of influence, including family, friends, neighbors, townspeople, and we were not going to be able to put a muzzle on that conversation either. In fact, we knew that what our employees had to say about the organization was going to be more highly trusted than our official spokespersons and if we told them they were prohibited, that's what they'd say to the media, friends, family, neighbors. To our ears, that sounded like we didn't trust them to get the spin right.

But we *did* trust them to get the truth right, so why not authorize them to tell the truth? Our employees could be our best ambassadors if empowered to do so. So we empowered them to talk about what they had witnessed or knew for sure. The only rule was that they were not authorized to spread rumors. Once the line of questioning got beyond the first-hand information they had on the subject, we recommended they forward the questioner to someone more directly involved in the response to make sure they got the facts. And then we made sure managers were clear that was our policy and were set up to keep their employees up to speed on any emergencies as they progressed so employees could pass on facts along with their endorsements that we were doing the right thing.

I'm not saying it will work for everyone, but I noticed that employee testimonials for the company really began making a difference. They were proud of the company and the work they did and weren't afraid to say so.

10.9 Begin Immediately to Shape the Narrative

Start talking about the crisis immediately, even when you think you have nothing specific to say. If you don't begin to shape the narrative, others will step in to fill the void and the information they provide may be downright inaccurate.

In December 2016, Edgar Maddison Welch drove from NC to Washington DC to "investigate" rumors (armed with an assault rifle) that Hillary Clinton was running a child sex ring out of the basement of the Comet Ping Pong Pizzeria.

According to Comet Pizza owner, James Alefantis, Comet Pizza does not even have a basement, but that did not stop the "Pizzagate" fake-news-driven conspiracy theory from exploding across social media sites. More than one million #PizzaGate tweets, including tweets from a number of political bots, contributed to undermining Hillary Clinton's campaign leading up to the 2016 presidential election.[149]

Also, during Arkema's Crosby TX crisis in 2017, the media sought out experts to explain the technical properties of organic peroxides and to weigh in with their opinions, even some who knew nothing about the situation and were espousing misinformed assumptions.

In the example below, one MIT professor disdainfully proclaimed the plant should not have even been operating.

It wasn't operating. The plant had shut down more than a week earlier, before Hurricane Harvey even made landfall because plant management was well aware the plant should batten down the hatches if there was a possibility of power loss.

Fig. 10-18. Ill-informed analysts will fill voids at
https://www.youtube.com/watch?v=_82Tf1x18n0

This was unfortunate because the company had been communicating since before the incident occurred and had processes in place to channel media questions so that accurate information could be provided.

A few years earlier – same company, different situation – a tote (plastic container for transporting chemicals) of ethyl acrylate slipped off a forklift and burst on impact with the ground. Just that small amount of product was so odiferous it could be smelled from the outskirts of Philadelphia all the way across the Delaware River into New Jersey, several miles away. Plant management immediately reported the incident since they recognized it was very likely to get media attention. Because of the early warning, we had enough time to get a few facts and identify that the business unit's manufacturing director was on site. I asked him to station himself in a conference room along with a couple of technical experts to assist as necessary.

By the time I received the first media phone call, I was able to provide the following facts:

- The product involved was ethyl acrylate. It is a raw material used in the manufacture of plastics. It has a strong odor and can be smelled even in very low quantities.

212

- Plant personnel immediately cleaned up the spill but there could be lingering odors.
- For any situation where those impacted believed they may be experiencing medical symptoms, whether we believed the situation warranted it, they should seek medical treatment.

But I am not an expert on ethyl acrylate and I didn't want the media to have to resort to uninformed "experts" or eyewitnesses because they'd reached the limits of my knowledge. My coup de grace was the ability to finish up by explaining that I had the business unit's manufacturing director on standby to answer any further questions and I'd be happy to patch him through.

The end result was that of the news stories posted, only one had an error (and it was relatively minor).

Arkema Inc.
Bristol, PA

June 10, 2014 – 11:30 A.M. Eastern

Tote spill at ARKEMA Bristol, PA site

There was a spill from a container of ethyl acrylate on-site at the Altuglas plant at Bristol, PA that occurred at approximately 8:30 A.M. Plant personnel immediately cleaned up the spill but there may be lingering odors.

Ethyl acrylate is a raw material used in the manufacture of plastics. It has a strong odor and can be smelled even in very low quantities. It can cause eye, skin or respiratory tract irritation.

If you believe you are experiencing medical symptoms or physical discomfort due to personal exposure to the ethyl acrylate from Bristol, PA this morning, Arkema recommends that you immediately seek medical treatment.

Arkema is cooperating with local authorities and an investigation will be performed.

Manufacturing Director Mark Heldt is available for questions.

*This Press Statement is made as part of Arkema's **Common Ground**® program. ARKEMA is committed to briefing its local partners about incidents at its sites and has pledged to manage its business in accordance with the principles of Responsible Care ®.*

*A global chemical company and France's leading chemicals producer, **Arkema** is building the future of the chemical industry every day. Deploying a responsible, innovation-based approach, we produce state-of-the-art specialty chemicals that provide customers with practical solutions to such challenges as climate change, access to drinking water, the future of energy, fossil fuel preservation and the need for lighter materials. With operations in more than 40 countries, some 14,000 employees and 10 research centers, Arkema generates annual revenue of approximately $8.1 billion, and holds leadership positions in all its markets with a portfolio of internationally recognized brands.*

Contact :
Mark Heldt   Tel. : 215-826-2742   E-mail : mark.heldt@arkema.com
Bristol
100 PA Rt. 413
Bristol, PA 19007

www.arkema.com

Fig. 10-19. Press release issued June 10, 2014.

214

Set yourself up for success by preparing in advance what it will take to be ready to begin communicating with accurate information immediately. Don't wait until you have gathered all the facts and gotten them approved and formatted as a press release. The media won't wait to start broadcasting the rumors they have gathered in the interim.

10.10 Holding Statements

Within reason, approve what you can approve *before* something happens.

Holding statements are generic statements or templates for creating statements that are meant to buy time by tiding the press over for the short term. They often say little more than that there has been an incident and we are responding.

We had multiple generic holding statements that any plant manager was authorized to tailor on the spot without waiting for "approvals," because they had already been approved by the chief legal counsel. These included a generic version of the statement above as well as rough outlines for the most basic of situations.

In the past, the gripe I'd most gotten from on-scene personnel was that it could take three hours for a statement to be approved by headquarters and they felt foolish with hands tied unable to provide the most basic information. It was simply not sustainable.

But the more the locations and business units tried to script statements in advance for every possible situation (blizzard, fire, product tampering), the more problematic approving holding statements got. The chief counsel put his foot down when one business unit (in all seriousness) took it as far as attempting to script a holding statement for "embezzlement." After all, if the business unit thought there was a high enough chance that an embezzlement holding statement could be needed, our best first step was probably to take a look at why that seemed a plausible risk and address the issue directly!

The reason the holding statements worked was primarily because they were so basic they could be tailored for just about any situation.

("_____ happened. We are taking the following steps. We will provide additional information where/when.")

10.10.1 Exercise: Amtrak Train Crash in Philadelphia (May 12, 2015)

When Amtrak President and CEO Joe Boardman delivered "A Message From Amtrak,"[150] it was well crafted, with an apology for the tragedy, thanks for those who stepped up, explanation of the action steps Amtrak is taking to assist the families as well as a commitment towards action to prevent this from ever happening again. However, this "Message from Amtrak" came three days after the event.

Question for Further Thought and Discussion:

> ➤ *Is there anything in paragraphs 1, 2 and 6 that couldn't have been said within an hour of the crash?*

Fig. 10-20. Amtrak press release three days after the crash.

In the interim, communication was framed by passengers who immediately began sharing what happened via social media… and speculation by non-Amtrak "experts" that the accident could have been the result of failing infrastructure or an engineer asleep at the switch, impaired or distracted.

10.11 Don't Panic

Never say "don't panic." People don't see themselves as panicking. They believe they are taking rational steps to protect themselves and their families, based on the information they have at their disposal. Withholding information drives people to uninformed sources. It is condescending and unrealistic to assume those impacted by a scary situation can be calmed with "trust us" – especially if the organization encouraging stakeholders to trust them is the same organization that caused the problem in the first place.

Instead, provide information and specific action steps they can take. For most, not having a say in decision-making and not being trusted with information cause panic; the antidote is more information not less.

While people are seeking information they are not acting helpless or panicking, so reach out early with a message of empathy and action.

- To the public, not knowing seems worse than dealing with a bad result.
- But early in a crisis typically there are more questions than answers.
- To combat: share the process you are using to get the answers.
- Tell the public what you know.
- Tell them also what you don't know, as well as how you are going about getting the answers[151].

10.12 Stakeholders

Identify in advance your key stakeholders or the most important audiences for you to communicate with so when the time comes, you will know who you need to reach out to.

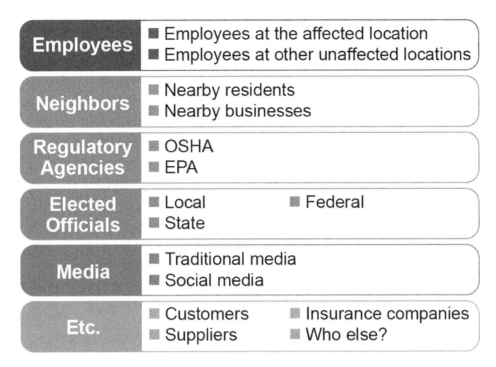

Employees	■ Employees at the affected location ■ Employees at other unaffected locations
Neighbors	■ Nearby residents ■ Nearby businesses
Regulatory Agencies	■ OSHA ■ EPA
Elected Officials	■ Local ■ Federal ■ State
Media	■ Traditional media ■ Social media
Etc.	■ Customers ■ Insurance companies ■ Suppliers ■ Who else?

Fig. 10-21. Key stakeholders.

Identify who the spokespersons for each key group will be. Rather than establishing relationships with media contacts, consider focusing the same amount of effort on establishing relationships with other key stakeholders who remain stakeholders for longer.

A journalist may remain in place for two years at the same station. A community member may live next to your facility for many years. What are the opportunities to build relationships with the community? Who are the key influencers or advocates? Who can you rely on to speak positively on your behalf? Those influencers who are more widely trusted than your key spokesperson(s) can be worth their weight in gold. Make sure you know who they are and have established a means to keep them up to date. Don't forget employees.

Only a small percentage of the population will likely fall into the realm of advocates. (Think in terms of your mother. No matter what you do, she's going to have your back and think you are the most talented, brightest person she's ever met. No matter what someone says about you, they're not going to change her mind.) Similarly, a small number of people may be adversaries. The vast majority will likely be ambivalent.[152]

Spend your time empowering the advocates to speak on your behalf. Inform and be courteous to the adversaries but don't spend a great deal of time trying to change their minds – it just may not be possible. Instead, work to neutralize any misinformation they spread. Counter with the information those who are ambivalent need in order to come to the conclusion on their own that what you have to say is reasonable and trustworthy. Your primary goal with ambivalent people is to keep them where they are in neutral territory (or slightly to the positive) so that the adversaries don't pull them into their camp.

10.12.1 Ghoul or Effigy? – A Case Study in Nudging Ambivalence

In October 2017, a Halloween decoration meant to look like a ghoul hanging from a tree limb was interpreted as a "racist display" representing "an effigy of a black person being lynched" according to one offended neighbor. The neighbor petitioned the homeowners' association with a request that the item be removed.

Rather than acting quickly and decisively, the homeowner replied "It is not my intent to offend anyone... I never realized the Monster in the tree had darker skin. If you see it up close it is indeed a Monster with blood clawed head and face... I have my entire garage full of items I am frantically preparing for Halloween and will spend most of the day Tuesday [Halloween day] setting up for Halloween. I can't promise I will have it down by Halloween but I can promise you this – I will NEVER ever put it up again."

The homeowner ultimately did take the item down before Halloween but that was not enough to satisfy the neighbor, who responded by posting a flier with a photo of a real lynching from 1889 next to the removed decoration and the family's address and labeling the family as racist.

Saying that he'd comply soon rather than immediately may have indicated a lack of sincerity in the apology. But it is likely no apology would have been sufficient in the eyes of an adversary whose intention was to pull neighborhood ambivalents out of neutral and into an opinion.[153]

Here is the photo taken by neighbor Jamie Stevenson and published in the Washington Post. Judge for yourself. Ghoul or effigy? Are you ambivalent after seeing it or have you been pulled left or right of neutral?

Fig. 10-22. Ghoul or effigy? You decide. *https://www.washingtonpost.com/local/a-halloween-display-or-a-faux-lynching-a-hanging-figure-creates-tensions-in-a-suburban-neighborhood/2017/10/31/62bdf8d2-be67-11e7-97d9-bdab5a0ab381_story.html?utm_term=.019c019e4d19*

Lesson learned: ambivalents don't really care one way or the other... until you give them a reason to take sides.

10.12.2 Florida Strawberry Fumigation – Another Case Study in Nudging Ambivalence

After toxic (but odorless) methyl bromide was outlawed, Florida strawberry growers began turning to Paladin™ to fumigate their soil prior to planting in 2014 and 2015. The chemical, developed and sold by Arkema, has the toxicity of garlic but its pungency can turn the stomach. Despite overwhelming scientific evidence of Paladin's™ safety,[154] a half dozen adversaries refused to back down from their certainty that it was Paladin™ that was making them sick, even though many of the complainants were in proximity to strawberry fields that were being fumigated with chemicals *other* than Paladin™ and where the nearest applications were miles away.

There were only a small number of very vocal adversaries, but they were able to attract skewed and inaccurate media coverage for their assertions.[155]

No amount of evidence was ever going to dissuade the adversaries. In a case like this, the best that can be done is to attempt to prevent ambivalents from being led by the nose into their crazy and media-fueled allegations.[156]

BY ANDREW HORVATH
Special to The Tampa Tribune
Published: September 5, 2015

I am writing this letter in response to Yvette Hammett's Aug. 30 article "Neighbors raise stink over strawberry pesticide" (front page). The article is biased toward a small number of Hillsborough residents who have made a number of unsubstantiated claims for the past two strawberry seasons.

The article is about a product called Paladin. The Paladin product is based on Dimethyl Disulfide, a naturally occurring compound found in many foods: garlic, cheese, milk, broccoli and others.

We have addressed many frequently asked questions at: www.Paladin.com/Questions-Florida.

The Paladin product does have a low odor threshold, but as confirmed by the Florida Department of Health, "Detecting an odor does not mean that harmful amounts of DMDS are being inhaled."

The Florida Department of Health report released earlier this year actually stated that there were zero cases of "confirmed" pesticide poisoning, and zero cases of "probable" pesticide poisoning.

Some of the individuals Ms. Hammett references as reporting health concerns to the Florida Department of Health have done so prior to the use of the Paladin product in the area. In these circumstances, it is absolutely impossible that our product was the cause for any health concerns. The disconnect between the timing of the alleged health concerns and product use was clearly communicated to Ms. Hammett during her tour of Mr. Young's fields last week.

Further, Ms. Hammett stated that "... farmers were ordered by the Florida Department of Agriculture and Consumer Affairs to switch to a thicker, impermeable plastic sheeting to cover the raised planting beds, to ensure that very little Paladin escapes." In truth, this change in practice was proactively driven by Arkema, and approved by FDACS. The change in practice was done after the new film technology was fully evaluated and confirmed a safe and beneficial practice for all stakeholders.

No one lives closer to these fields than Mr. Young and his family. Arkema and Mr. Young have made a consistent effort to be responsible stewards of the land and air and have made efforts to address any concerns expressed by community members.

All applications have fully complied with the label and have used good agricultural practices, deploying the most technically sophisticated equipment in the market. Arkema invested more than 10 years in researching the safety of the product before receiving our U.S. and Florida labels. Arkema's Paladin product stewardship program is one of the most advanced and complete programs in the United States.

Andrew Horvath is business manager for Arkema.

Fig. 10-23. Letter to the editor September 5, 2015 published in the Tampa Tribune.

Lesson learned: provide ambivalents with the information they need in order to conclude on their own that what you have to say is reasonable and trustable. Your primary goal is to keep them neutral so adversaries don't get a foothold.

10.12.3 Exercise: Tulsa Solkatronic[157]

Read through the short summary below and identify the key stakeholders with whom Tulsa Solkatronic should have been coordinating and communicating in advance of this emergency.

- Tulsa Port of Catoosa workers say they were exposed to arsine gas, a derivative of arsenic, for an unnecessarily long period of time, and they're worried about the possible long-term effects of the prolonged exposure.
- A tank of the toxic gas exploded at the inland port and sent more than 100 people to five Tulsa-area hospitals and prompted a flurry of evacuations.
- After the tank erupted at the Solkatronic Chemical plant, workers at the neighboring Air-X-Changers building stood outside for more than an hour in the gas's dangerous fumes. The workers say they didn't move until a firefighter learned about the gas's danger and advised them to leave.
- A Solkatronic employee stood on a truck and told them they had indeed been exposed to a very hazardous material and might need medical attention. Until then, the workers say, they had no idea that they had been working next door to dangerous chemicals.
- More than 100 people, including many employees and subcontractors working at Solkatronic and Air-X-Changers, were hospitalized for one to two days.
- One of the Air-X-Changers bosses told employees to "'*stay right here.' We were right there where the fumes were coming right toward us. They should have moved us to a different facility instead of just having to sit outside there.*"
- Adding to the frustration has been a lack of information provided since the incident.

- *"Our company and (Solkatronic) hasn't said nothing to nobody. They're keeping us all in the dark. I think that's pretty wrong, after you gas somebody you don't say nothing to them."*
- Air-X-Changers management had no comment on the workers' concerns and refused to take any further questions. A spokeswoman with Solkatronic's Pennsylvania headquarters also declined comment.
- The gas causes respiratory problems and can destroy a victim's red blood cells. It is potentially lethal.
- Although authorities considered closing the port, sirens never sounded. The port employs several thousand people, officials said.

Questions for Further Thought and Discussion

- ➤ *Who are the key audiences?*
- ➤ *If you were Tulsa Solkatronic and could go back in time, what information would you have exchanged with these key audiences? How would you have done it?*
- ➤ *What is the benefit of doing this in advance rather than waiting and hoping an emergency doesn't occur? (Tip: What were the stakeholders' issues as a result of this emergency and how could Tulsa Solkatronic have diffused those issues with up front information?)*

10.13 Emergency Notification

Many crisis plans have a section with contact lists and phone trees with the intention that if there is an emergency, information can be disseminated through a series of daisy chains. Be cautious, however, because any broken link in the daisy chain can cause a break in being able to carry out team communications.

Consider whether you can automate team lists so phone numbers don't have to be checked manually and transposed a couple of times a year to keep them relevant. Are you posting these numbers in more than one place, such as a human resources database and also in the crisis plan? If so, you've now just doubled the chances that when someone's number changes or is updated, it will be missed or incorrect in other locations.

Who has been assigned to call the crisis team together when a crisis has been identified? And how long will this take (especially if the administrative assistant tasked with pulling everyone together isn't immediately available or it's a weekend or after hours)? Are there multiple people and clear thresholds (see section 6.2) for determining what requires convening the crisis team? Can the notification be sent through automated means rather than a series of phone calls?

There are a lot of automated or subscription crisis notification systems, services and apps available in a broad range of prices and capabilities. Identify which best serves your organization's needs. Use them to convene the crisis team, provide short updates or critical information to affected personnel. Some systems allow two-way communication so you can employ your entire workforce as signal detectors.

One word of caution on this: in one organization I worked for, employees became accustomed to getting emergency notifications directly to their cell phones from the global security operations center (GSOC) whenever there was a scheduled tornado shelter-in-place drill. It never occurred to employees when a real tornado closed in, that the reason they didn't hear about it was because no one on site thought to alert the GSOC (located in another region) so that the information could be communicated.

Be sure as you adopt new tools to test them realistically and ensure full awareness that there's still an element of human fallibility.

Summary

You're committed to start communicating quickly in a crisis, including with and through social media. You've crafted your hip pocket statements to facilitate achieving that goal. You've analyzed how to get stakeholders to positive information, build your credibility within your community, and are prepared to break your own bad news rather than letting anyone else frame your story. You've developed your concept of operations and built your team. You've put signal detectors in place, considered the role of apology, and practiced your spokesperson techniques.

This final chapter wrapped things up with logistics for small organizations with limited communications staff, the role of the crisis wingman, strategies for winning the game, effective messaging and bridging techniques, communication strategies with victims, using employees as spokespersons, and shaping the narrative.

Questions for Further Thought and Discussion

➢ *What actionable information might your organization need to get out in real time in a crisis? How can you use your organization's social media tools to do so?*

➢ *If yours is a smaller organization with limited communications staff, what will be your go-to set-up for recording a statement via video clip? (Review section 10.2.) What logistics will you need to put in place in advance so you are ready on the spur of the moment? Do a dry run.*

➢ *Think through a recent situation where you needed to give an interview. What were the two or three key points you needed to get across? Did the reporter ask the right questions? If not, rethink the conversation to armchair-quarterback how you could have bridged to your message points from the questions the reporter asked.*

➢ *Could you have used a wingman in this situation? If so, how could you have achieved a better effect?*

➢ *Who are the key stakeholders for your organization? Is there just one spokesperson for your organization or are there multiple liaisons who can focus on communicating key messages simultaneously with their identified audiences?*

CONCLUSION

I spend my professional life building resilience by working with otherwise extremely savvy executives who know how to run a business profitably and efficiently but who often plan to either run a crisis by the seat of their pants or to delegate both crisis communication and crisis management to public relations consultants.

The best outcome – bar none – instead occurs when executives take the time to delve into preparing for the likelihood that someday their organization will face a potential crisis that could derail everything they've built if not managed as carefully as they've planned out every other strategy in their enterprise.

Good crisis management doesn't occur by chance and it doesn't happen on the day of the crisis. It is built on a strong foundation, with a mission focused on doing the right thing without obfuscation. A team is carefully selected (in advance). Stakeholders who matter are identified and positioned to be kept in the know. Statements are wordsmithed not to sound good, but with information that answers their questions and focus on what the organization is doing to right the situation for the impacted parties and ensure the problem never happens again.

EXECUTING CRISIS, provides the strategies necessary for your organization's leaders to take crisis management from a theoretical exercise mired in "best practices" that are outdated and unrealistic for today's environment, and makes them tangible and useable.

These are the *new* rules for crisis leadership:

- Communicate at the speed of sound.
- Craft your hip-pocket statements now. Today. Really. Don't wait until you are in a crisis to figure out what you are going to say. Doing it right now is the only way you'll be able to begin communicating at the speed of sound.
- Traditional media have embraced and embedded social media in their communication about crisis. So should you. Social media can spread misinformation and rumors globally within minutes. You will never catch up or set the record straight if you don't acknowledge social media's power and plan to harness it.
- Choose your spokespersons carefully and make sure they are well prepped.
- "Trust us" only works once. When you say it, mean it.
- Official spokespersons are not always the most reliable. Build alliances with unofficial spokespersons who can speak credibly on your behalf.
- Take one step beyond what stakeholders really expect. It will lessen the sting of the impact you have caused.
- Break your own story. Shape your own narrative. Get out ahead of the speculation.
- Make good news easy to find.
- Be a good neighbor.
- No successful crisis begins on the day of the crisis. Build your plan, team and strategies in advance. Tailor a solution that works for your unique circumstances.
- Streamline your approval process.
- Armchair quarterback (in advance) where the train could jump the tracks.

- Challenge experts' "cardinal rules." Ensure "best practice" is best for *your* organization.
- Adjust your corporate culture to report problems rather than wait and hope they don't come to light.
- Identify the signal detectors that can warn you in advance that a crisis is brewing and create a process to channel the input to a volume that can be heard by the right receptors.
- An apology – done well – can go a long way towards healing a rift and mitigating the possibility of a lawsuit, whereas an apology done badly can pour gas on a flame.
- Answer reporter questions in 20 seconds or three sentences.
- Determine what information your key stakeholders need and how to get it into their hands quickly.
- Spend time with your trusted advisors anticipating questions and developing answers before a press conference or interview. Identify a crisis wingman who will have your back.
- Winning the game may require reframing the issue. Bridge to the answers you need to impart even if the right questions don't get asked. Don't keep volleying once you have won the game.
- Identify affected parties and assist them in bringing closure to the incident.

Today's executive needs to be prepared to take quick action to annihilate potential crises before they happen. EXECUTING CRISIS provides the guidance needed for executing on that need.

ENDNOTES

[1] Wilcox, D.L. & Cameron, G. T. (2006). *Public Relations: Strategies and Tactics* (edition 8), chapter 6. Boston: Pearson Education Inc.

[2] Janofsky, M. (1997, July 8). Three Workers Found Killed in Coffee Shop in Georgetown" *New York Times*.
http://www.nytimes.com/1997/07/08/us/three-workers-found-killed-in-coffee-shop-in-georgetown.html

[3] http://www.nytimes.com/2014/11/16/us/four-workers-are-killed-in-gas-leak-at-texas-chemical-plant.html?_r=2

[4]   http://www.dupont.com/corporate-functions/media-center/press-releases/dupont-news-statement-on-laporte-texas-facility-incident.html
Also on Wayback Machine archive at
https://web.archive.org/web/20141118011508/http://www.dupont.com/corporate-functions/media-center/press-releases/dupont-news-statement-on-laporte-texas-facility-incident.html

[5] http://www.actua.com/fatal-toxic-gas-leak-reinforces-critical-need-greater-employee-community-protections/
https://www.whitehouse.gov/the-press-office/2013/08/01/executive-order-improving-chemical-facility-safety-and-security

[6] Fernandez, L. & Merzer, M. (2003). *Jane's Crisis Communications Handbook: A Guide to Emergency Media Relations for Information Officers, First Responders and the Press.* Edition 1. Alexandria VA: Jane's Information Group.

[7] Centers for Disease Control [CDC] (2014 edition). Crisis and Emergency Risk Communication. Available online at:
https://www.google.com/url?sa=t&rct=j&q=&esrc=s&source=web&cd=1&cad=rja&uact=8&ved=2ahUKEwjl1-yH3eLiAhVShuAKHVXjBcAQFjAAegQIABAC&url=https%3A%2F%2Femergency.cdc.gov%2Fcerc%2Fresources%2Fpdf%2Fcerc_2014edition.pdf&usg=AOvVaw2SGMgqsJk0QvMSEuAz3mZQ
Also, CDC. Crisis and Emergency Risk Communication... For Leaders By Leaders. Available online at: http://emergency.cdc.gov/erc/leaders.pdf

[8] Fernandez, L. & Merzer, M. (2003). *Jane's Crisis Communications Handbook: A Guide to Emergency Media Relations for Information Officers, First Responders and the Press.* Edition 1. Alexandria VA: Jane's Information Group.

[9] Fernandez, L. & Merzer, M. (2003). *Jane's Crisis Communications Handbook: A Guide to Emergency Media Relations for Information Officers, First Responders and the Press.* Edition 1. Alexandria VA: Jane's Information Group.

[10] Fernandez, L. & Merzer, M. (2003). *Jane's Crisis Communications Handbook: A Guide to Emergency Media Relations for Information Officers, First Responders and the Press.* Edition 1. Alexandria VA: Jane's Information Group.

[11] Fernandez, L. & Merzer, M. (2003). *Jane's Crisis Communications Handbook: A Guide to Emergency Media Relations for Information Officers, First Responders and the Press.* Edition 1. Alexandria VA: Jane's Information Group.

[12] Fernandez, L. & Merzer, M. (2003). *Jane's Crisis Communications Handbook: A Guide to Emergency Media Relations for Information Officers, First Responders and the Press.* Edition 1. Alexandria VA: Jane's Information Group.

[13] Pew Research Center surveys and Statista. http://www.pewinternet.org/2016/11/11/social-media-update-2016/ https://www.statista.com/statistics/259477/hours-of-video-uploaded-to-youtube-every-minute/

[14] https://newsroom.fb.com/company-info/

[15] https://www.statista.com/statistics/259477/hours-of-video-uploaded-to-youtube-every-minute/

[16] https://www.socialmediatoday.com/marketing/how-much-time-do-people-spend-social-media-infographic

[17] https://wearesocial.com/global-digital-report-2019 and https://www.slideshare.net/wearesocialsg/digital-in-2016/160-wearesocialsg_160JAN2016_TOP_ACTIVE_SOCIAL

[18] https://managementhelp.org/blogs/crisis-management/2012/06/10/asus-fails-at-social-media/

[19] https://melissaagnes.com/the-secret-to-successful-crisis-management-in-the-21st-century/

[20] http://www.washingtonpost.com/wp-dyn/content/article/2006/12/11/AR2006121101539.html

[21] http://www.washingtonpost.com/wp-dyn/content/article/2006/12/13/AR2006121301686.html

[22] http://freerepublic.com/focus/f-chat/1805499/posts

[23] http://www.nytimes.com/1999/02/02/us/explosion-at-ford-plant-kills-worker.html
http://www.cnn.com/US/9902/02/ford.explosion.03/
https://www.newspapers.com/newspage/100179415/

[24] Lukaszewski, J. (2013). *Lukaszewski on Crisis Communication: What Your CEO Needs to Know About Reputation Risk and Crisis Management.* Brookfield CT: Rothstein Publishing. Pages 123-124.

[25] https://www.washingtonpost.com/news/wonk/wp/2015/12/09/chipotle-food-outbreak-ecoli-reputation/?utm_term=.8053f34ca179

https://www.washingtonpost.com/news/wonk/wp/2015/12/21/the-cdc-is-investigating-another-outbreak-that-could-be-linked-to-chipotle/?utm_term=.81f700f23d34

[26] http://www.houstonchronicle.com/chemical-breakdown/1/

[27] From Arkema's safe handling and use fact sheet for organic peroxides: http://www.luperox.com/export/sites/organicperoxide/.content/medias/downloads/literature/their-safe-handling-and-use.pdf

[28] Rich Rennard press conference clip
https://www.youtube.com/watch?v=RichBVHRcPY

Transcript of Rich Rennard press conference:

http://www.cnn.com/TRANSCRIPTS/1708/31/cnr.03.html

[29] Bureau of Labor Statistics
https://www.bls.gov/iif/oshsum.htm#16Summary_News_Release

[30] https://www.arkema.com/en/social-responsibility/industrial-safety/

[31] https://www.washingtonpost.com/news/energy-environment/wp/2017/09/04/chemical-companies-have-already-released-1-million-pounds-of-extra-air-pollutants-thanks-to-harvey/?utm_term=.b397ec27a1e0

[32] https://www.forbes.com/2001/06/20/tireindex.html#456d28273401

[33] https://www.nytimes.com/2016/12/20/us/flint-water-charges.html?_r=0
https://www.nytimes.com/news-event/flint-water-crisis
http://www.cnn.com/2016/03/04/us/flint-water-crisis-fast-facts/index.html

[34] https://fortune.com/2015/09/23/volkswagen-stock-drop/

[35] https://www.nytimes.com/2016/02/28/business/international/vws-crisis-strategy-forward-reverse-u-turn.html

[36] https://www.nytimes.com/2017/01/10/business/volkswagen-diesel-settlement.html

[37] https://www.nytimes.com/2017/02/01/business/bosch-vw-diesel-settlement.html

[38] https://www.washingtonpost.com/news/energy-environment/wp/2016/12/01/princess-cruises-to-pay-record-breaking-criminal-fine-for-ocean-pollution/?utm_term=.8bb9f038b366

[39] Robertson, J. (2012). Apology as a business decision. *Public Relations Journal.* 6 (1). https://prjournal.instituteforpr.org/wp-content/uploads/2012Robertson.pdf

[40] See National Incident Management Field Operations Guide https://www.fema.gov/media-library/assets/documents/84807

[41] NFPA 1600 Standard (chapter A.6.8.1) 2019 edition. https://www.nfpa.org/codes-and-standards/all-codes-and-standards/list-of-codes-and-standards/detail?code=1600

[42] Fernandez, L. & Merzer, M. (2003). *Jane's Crisis Communications Handbook: A Guide to Emergency Media Relations for Information Officers, First Responders and the Press.* Edition 1. Alexandria VA: Jane's Information Group.

[43] Ripley, A. (2009). *The Unthinkable: Who Survives When Disaster Strikes and Why.* New York: Three Rivers Press. Pages 203-210.

[44] Augustine, N.R. (2000). Managing the crisis you tried to prevent. *Harvard Business Review on Crisis Management.* Boston: Harvard Business School Publishing. Pages 1-31.

[45] https://www.nytimes.com/2018/01/08/business/apple-investors-children.html?mtrref=www.google.com&gwh=4A89E36345D86BB667E94A4C9B7CD423&gwt=pay

[46] http://www.philly.com/philly/news/nation_world/video-of-patient-put-out-in-the-cold-stirs-fury-20180111.html Also https://twitter.com/imamu_baraka?lang=en

[47] https://www.washingtonpost.com/opinions/i-survived-an-amtrak-crash-this-weeks-victims-are-in-for-a-rude-awakening/2017/12/20/b0e9af4e-e5a7-11e7-a65d-1ac0fd7f097e_story.html?utm_term=.a184305cb8ae

48 Robertson, J. (2012). Apology as a business decision. *Public Relations Journal.* 6 (1). https://prjournal.instituteforpr.org/wp-content/uploads/2012Robertson.pdf

49 NFPA 1600 Standard (chapter 5.2.2.1) 2019 edition. https://www.nfpa.org/codes-and-standards/all-codes-and-standards/list-of-codes-and-standards/detail?code=1600

50 https://www.pressreader.com/usa/the-washington-post-sunday/20160925/282218010270941

51 Fernandez, L. & Merzer, M. (2003). *Jane's Crisis Communications Handbook: A Guide to Emergency Media Relations for Information Officers, First Responders and the Press.* Edition 1. Alexandria VA: Jane's Information Group.

52 Centers for Disease Control [CDC] (2014 edition). Crisis and Emergency Risk Communication. Available online at: https://www.google.com/url?sa=t&rct=j&q=&esrc=s&source=web&cd=1&cad=rja&uact=8&ved=2ahUKEwjl1-yH3eLiAhVShuAKHVXjBcAQFjAAegQIABAC&url=https%3A%2F%2Femergency.cdc.gov%2Fcerc%2Fresources%2Fpdf%2Fcerc_2014edition.pdf&usg=AOvVaw2SGMgqsJk0QvMSEuAz3mZQ
Also, CDC. Crisis and Emergency Risk Communication… For Leaders By Leaders. Available online at: http://emergency.cdc.gov/erc/leaders.pdf

53 https://jobs.metlife.com/MLG/job/NY-Director%2C-Americas-Crisis-Management-NY-10166/450555800/ (captured 1/21/18) https://www.glassdoor.com/job-listing/business-continuity-management-vice-president-mitsubishi-ufj-financial-group-JV_IC1146832_KO0,45_KE46,76.htm?jl=2631584926 (captured 1/21/18) https://www.linkedin.com/jobs/view/vice-president%2C-risk-analysis-at-mastercard-565158918/ (captured 1/21/18)

[54] https://www.pressreader.com/usa/the-washington-post/20171123/281809989203451

[55] www.Bernsteincrisismanagement.com/protect-rep-uber-crisis-communications-done-wrong/

[56] Mitroff, I. with Anagnos, G. (2001). *Managing Crises Before They Happen: What Every Executive and Manager Needs to Know About Crisis Management*. New York: Amacom.

[57] https://money.cnn.com/1999/07/05/companies/q_coke/ and https://www.slideshare.net/abhizar/coca-cola-belgian-pr-crisis

[58] SafeStart https://www.safestart.com

[59] Bernard Roche, former CEO of Arkema Inc. The slogan referred to the total recordable incident rate (TRIR) generated each month and is multiplied by the number of personnel/manhours on site. Roche's aim was to strive for zero. During his tenure, Arkema Inc. got pretty close—at one point dipping below a TRIR of 1.5.

[60] http://www.startribune.com/the-norwood-teague-resignation-another-weak-phony-apology/321322951/

[61] https://www.pressreader.com/usa/the-washington-post/20171101/282248075822836

[62] Patel, A. & Reinsch, L. (2003, March). Companies <u>can</u> apologize: corporate apologies and legal liability. *Business Communication Quarterly*. 66 (1), 9-25.

[63] Buttny, R. (1993). *Social Accountability in Communication*. London: Sage Publications.

[64] Patel, A. & Reinsch, L. (2003, March). Companies <u>can</u> apologize: corporate apologies and legal liability. *Business Communication Quarterly.* 66 (1), 9-25.

[65] Holtgraves, T. (1989). The form and function of remedial moves: reported use, psychological reality, and perceived effectiveness. *Journal of Language and Social Psychology.* 8, 1-16.

[66] Holtgraves, T. (1989). The form and function of remedial moves: reported use, psychological reality, and perceived effectiveness. *Journal of Language and Social Psychology.* 8, 1-16.

[67] Benoit, W.L. (1995). *Accounts, Excuses, and Apologies: A Theory of Image Restoration Strategies.* Albany: State University of New York Press.

[68] https://www.pressreader.com/usa/the-washington-post/20170414/281616715236486

[69] http://observer.com/2017/04/united-airlines-dragged-passenger-10000-policy/

[70] https://www.nytimes.com/2017/04/11/business/united-airline-passenger-overbooked-flights.html

[71] https://www.washingtonpost.com/news/on-leadership/wp/2017/04/27/the-most-important-united-airlines-policy-change-after-its-dragging-fiasco-could-also-be-the-hardest/?utm_term=.0c104e674838

[72] Blumstein, P.W., et al. (1974). The honoring of accounts. *American Socialogical Review.* 39, 551-566.

[73] Benoit, W.L. (1995). *Accounts, Excuses, and Apologies: A Theory of Image Restoration Strategies*. Albany: State University of New York Press.

[74] Tavuchis, N. (1991). *Mea culpa: A Sociology of Apology and Reconciliation*. Stanford CA: Stanford University Press.

[75] Levi, D.L. (1997, November). The role of apology in mediation. *New York University Law Review*. 72, 1165-1210.

[76] Latif, E. (2001, February). Apologetic justice: evaluating apologies tailored toward legal solutions. *Boston University Law Review*. 81, 289-320.

[77] Bies, R.J. (1987). The predicament of injustice: the management of moral outrage. In Cummings, L.L. & Staw, B.M. (Eds.) *Research in Organizational Behavior: An Annual Series of Analytical Essays and Critical Reviews*. 9, 289-319. Greenwich CT: JAI Press Inc.

[78] Hearit, K.M. (1995, Spring/Summer). Mistakes were made: organizations, apologia, and crises of social legitimacy. *Communication Studies*. 46, 1-17.

[79] Hearit, K.M. (1995, Spring/Summer). Mistakes were made: organizations, apologia, and crises of social legitimacy. *Communication Studies*. 46, 1-17.

[80] Small, W.J. (1991). Exxon Valdez: how to spend billions and still get a black eye. *Public Relations Review*. 17 (1), 9-25.

[81] https://www.nytimes.com/2001/06/17/business/the-right-thing-a-blame-game-hurts-both-ford-and-firestone.html

[82] Wildgust, J. (2001, April 9). Crisis!: Firestone's tough lesson in PR mismanagement. *Public Relations*. p. 18.

[83] Fishman, D.A. (1999, Fall). ValuJet flight 592: crisis communication theory blended and extended. *Communication Quarterly*. 47 (4), 345-376.

[84] Yagoda, B. (1990, April). Cleaning up a dirty image. *Business Month*. pp. 48-51.

[85] Saffir, L. & Tarrant, J. (1993). *Power Public Relations: How to Get PR to Work for You*. Lincolnwood IL: NTC Publishing Group.

[86] Levi, D.L. (1997, November). The role of apology in mediation. *New York University Law Review*. 72, 1165-1210. And Wagatsuma, H. & Rosett, A. (1986). The implications of apology: law and culture in Japan and the United States. *Law & Society Review*. 20 (4), 461-498.

[87] Marcus, A.A. & Goodman, R.S. (1991, June). Victims and shareholders: the dilemmas of presenting corporate policy during a crisis. *The Academy of Management Journal*. 34 (2), 281-305.

[88] Martinelli, K.A. & Briggs, W. (1998). Integrating public relations and legal responses during a crisis: the case of Odwalla, Inc. *Public Relations Review*. 24 (4), 443-460. And Horsley, J.S. & Barker, R.T. (2002, October). Toward a synthesis model for crisis communication in the public sector: an initial investigation. *Journal of Business and Technical Communication*. 16 (4), 406-440.

[89] Cooper, D.A. (1992, January). CEO must weigh legal and public relations approaches. *The Public Relations Journal*. 48 (1), 40-41.

[90] Cohen, J.R. (1999, May). Advising clients to apologize. *Southern California Law Review*. 72, 1009.

[91] Sellnow, T.L. & Ulmer, R.R. (1995, Winter). Ambiguous argument as advocacy in organizational crisis communication. *Argumentation & Advocacy*. 31 (3), 138-150.

[92] Martinelli, K.A. & Briggs, W. (1998). Integrating public relations and legal responses during a crisis: the case of Odwalla, Inc. *Public Relations Review*. 24 (4), 443-460.

[93] Marra, F.J. (1998). Crisis communication plans: poor predictors of excellent crisis public relations. *Public Relations Review*. 24 (4) 461-474.

[94] Ucelli, L. (2002). The CEO's 'how to' guide to crisis communications. *Strategy & Leadership*. 30 (2), 21-24.

[95] Nelson-Horchler, J. (1990, Apr 16). We were wrong: acts of contrition brighten a company's tarnished image. *Industry Week*. 239 (8), 20-26.

[96] Kaufmann, J.B., Kesner, I.F., & Hazan, T.L. (1994). The myth of full disclosure: a look at organizational communications during crisis. *Business Horizons*. 37, (4), 29-39.

[97] Frank, J. (2000, October). A spate of corporate crises in the US has seen CEOs take centre stage to personally apologise to their customers. *PR Week*. p. 36.

[98] Cohen, J.R. (1999, May). Advising clients to apologize. *Southern California Law Review*. 72, 1009. And Levi, D.L. (1997, November). The role of apology in mediation. *New York University Law Review*. 72, 1165-1210.

[99] Coombs, W.T. & Holladay, S.J. (2002, November). Helping crisis managers protect reputational assets: initial tests of the situational crisis

communication theory. *Management Communication Quarterly*. 16 (2), 165-186.

[100] Coombs, W.T. & Holladay, S.J. (2002, November). Helping crisis managers protect reputational assets: initial tests of the situational crisis communication theory. *Management Communication Quarterly*. 16 (2), 165-186.

[101] Coombs, W.T. (1995, May). Choosing the right words: the development of guidelines for the selection of the "appropriate" crisis-response strategies. *Management Communication Quarterly*. 8 (4), 447-476.

[102] Benoit, W.L. & Brinson, S.L. (1994, Winter). AT&T: apologies are not enough. *Communication Quarterly*. 42 (1), 75. And Brinson, S.L. & Benoit, W.L. (1996, Winter). Dow Corning's image repair strategies in the breast implant crisis. *Communication Quarterly*. 44 (1), 29-38. And Fishman, D.A. (1999, Fall). ValuJet flight 592: crisis communication theory blended and extended. *Communication Quarterly*. 47 (4), 345-376.

[103] https://www.nytimes.com/2015/02/06/business/experts-suspect-lax-security-left-anthem-vulnerable-to-hackers.html

[104] https://www.washingtonpost.com/news/federal-eye/wp/2015/07/09/hack-of-security-clearance-system-affected-21-5-million-people-federal-authorities-say/

[105] https://www.pressreader.com/usa/the-washington-post/20170913/282033327360522

[106] Hearit, K.M. (2001). Corporate apologia: when an organization speaks in defense of itself. In Heath, R.L. (ed.) *Handbook of Public Relations*. Thousand Oaks, CA: Sage. Ch. 42, pp. 501-511.

[107] Sugimoto, N. (1997, August). A Japan-U.S. comparison of apology styles. *Communication Research*. pp. 349-369.

[108] Wagatsuma, H. & Rosett, A. (1986). The implications of apology: law and culture in Japan and the United States. *Law & Society Review*. 20 (4), 461-498.

[109] Wagatsuma, H. & Rosett, A. (1986). The implications of apology: law and culture in Japan and the United States. *Law & Society Review*. 20 (4), 461-498.

[110] Wagatsuma, H. & Rosett, A. (1986). The implications of apology: law and culture in Japan and the United States. *Law & Society Review*. 20 (4), 461-498.

[111] Swanson, D.J. (1985, August 15). For Japanese, lawsuits are the last resort. *The Dallas Morning News*. pp. 1A, 15A.

[112] Robertson, J. (2006). Apology as a business decision: an initial examination of accepted best practice in crisis communications. Unpublished dissertation. The George Washington University.

[113] Robertson, J. (2006). Apology as a business decision: an initial examination of accepted best practice in crisis communications. Unpublished dissertation. The George Washington University.

[114] Robertson, J. (2006). Apology as a business decision: an initial examination of accepted best practice in crisis communications. Unpublished dissertation. The George Washington University.

[115] Robertson, J. (2006). Apology as a business decision: an initial examination of accepted best practice in crisis communications. Unpublished dissertation. The George Washington University.

[116] http://www.melissaagnes.com/take-a-cue-from-browns-how-not-to-respond-to-a-social-media-crisis/

[117] Centers for Disease Control [CDC]. Crisis and Emergency Risk Communication… For Leaders By Leaders. Available online at: http://emergency.cdc.gov/erc/leaders.pdf

[118] Centers for Disease Control [CDC]. Crisis and Emergency Risk Communication… For Leaders By Leaders. Available online at: http://emergency.cdc.gov/erc/leaders.pdf

[119] Centers for Disease Control [CDC]. Crisis and Emergency Risk Communication… For Leaders By Leaders. Available online at: http://emergency.cdc.gov/erc/leaders.pdf

[120] Centers for Disease Control [CDC]. Crisis and Emergency Risk Communication… For Leaders By Leaders. Available online at: http://emergency.cdc.gov/erc/leaders.pdf

[121] Centers for Disease Control [CDC]. Crisis and Emergency Risk Communication… For Leaders By Leaders. Available online at: http://emergency.cdc.gov/erc/leaders.pdf

[122] Centers for Disease Control [CDC]. Crisis and Emergency Risk Communication… For Leaders By Leaders. Available online at: http://emergency.cdc.gov/erc/leaders.pdf

[123] Centers for Disease Control [CDC]. Crisis and Emergency Risk Communication… For Leaders By Leaders. Available online at: http://emergency.cdc.gov/erc/leaders.pdf

[124] Centers for Disease Control [CDC]. Crisis and Emergency Risk Communication… For Leaders By Leaders. Available online at: http://emergency.cdc.gov/erc/leaders.pdf

[125] Centers for Disease Control [CDC]. Crisis and Emergency Risk Communication... For Leaders By Leaders. Available online at: http://emergency.cdc.gov/erc/leaders.pdf

[126] Centers for Disease Control [CDC]. Crisis and Emergency Risk Communication... For Leaders By Leaders. Available online at: http://emergency.cdc.gov/erc/leaders.pdf

[127] Lydersen, K. (2007, June 21). University accused of lying to hide killing. *The Washington Post*. http://www.washingtonpost.com/wp-dyn/content/article/2007/06/20/AR2007062002172.html

[128] Zamiska, N. (2007, June 21). Wyeth accused of secret recall. *The Washington Post*. https://www.pressreader.com/usa/the-washington-post/20070621/282664682972259

[129] https://www.washingtonpost.com/news/food/wp/2017/09/11/a-pizza-hut-told-irma-fleeing-employees-they-could-be-punished-for-skipping-shifts/?utm_term=.5616ba9fc2d1

[130] https://www.washingtonpost.com/news/worldviews/wp/2017/09/12/marriott-sent-a-rescue-ship-to-the-caribbean-after-irma-and-left-non-guests-on-the-dock/?utm_term=.14ad44990d32

[131] https://www.ocregister.com/2016/04/06/ex-coal-ceo-gets-1-year-in-prison-in-deadly-west-virginia-mine-blast/

[132] Centers for Disease Control [CDC] (2014 edition). Crisis and Emergency Risk Communication. Available online at: https://www.google.com/url?sa=t&rct=j&q=&esrc=s&source=web&cd=1&cad=rja&uact=8&ved=2ahUKEwjl1-yH3eLiAhVShuAKHVXjBcAQFjAAegQIABAC&url=https%3A%2F%2

Femergency.cdc.gov%2Fcerc%2Fresources%2Fpdf%2Fcerc_2014edition.
pdf&usg=AOvVaw2SGMgqsJk0QvMSEuAz3mZQ
Also, CDC. Crisis and Emergency Risk Communication… For Leaders By
Leaders. Available online at: http://emergency.cdc.gov/erc/leaders.pdf

[133] Centers for Disease Control [CDC] (2014 edition). Crisis and
Emergency Risk Communication. Available online at:
https://www.google.com/url?sa=t&rct=j&q=&esrc=s&source=web&cd=1
&cad=rja&uact=8&ved=2ahUKEwjl1-
yH3eLiAhVShuAKHVXjBcAQFjAAegQIABAC&url=https%3A%2F%2
Femergency.cdc.gov%2Fcerc%2Fresources%2Fpdf%2Fcerc_2014edition.
pdf&usg=AOvVaw2SGMgqsJk0QvMSEuAz3mZQ
Also, CDC. Crisis and Emergency Risk Communication… For Leaders By
Leaders. Available online at: http://emergency.cdc.gov/erc/leaders.pdf

[134] Centers for Disease Control [CDC] (2014 edition). Crisis and
Emergency Risk Communication. Available online at:
https://www.google.com/url?sa=t&rct=j&q=&esrc=s&source=web&cd=1
&cad=rja&uact=8&ved=2ahUKEwjl1-
yH3eLiAhVShuAKHVXjBcAQFjAAegQIABAC&url=https%3A%2F%2
Femergency.cdc.gov%2Fcerc%2Fresources%2Fpdf%2Fcerc_2014edition.
pdf&usg=AOvVaw2SGMgqsJk0QvMSEuAz3mZQ
Also, CDC. Crisis and Emergency Risk Communication… For Leaders By
Leaders. Available online at: http://emergency.cdc.gov/erc/leaders.pdf

[135] Centers for Disease Control [CDC] (2014 edition). Crisis and
Emergency Risk Communication. Available online at:
https://www.google.com/url?sa=t&rct=j&q=&esrc=s&source=web&cd=1
&cad=rja&uact=8&ved=2ahUKEwjl1-
yH3eLiAhVShuAKHVXjBcAQFjAAegQIABAC&url=https%3A%2F%2
Femergency.cdc.gov%2Fcerc%2Fresources%2Fpdf%2Fcerc_2014edition.
pdf&usg=AOvVaw2SGMgqsJk0QvMSEuAz3mZQ
Also, CDC. Crisis and Emergency Risk Communication… For Leaders By
Leaders. Available online at: http://emergency.cdc.gov/erc/leaders.pdf

[136] Fernandez, L. & Merzer, M. (2003). *Jane's Crisis Communications Handbook: A Guide to Emergency Media Relations for Information Officers, First Responders and the Press.* Edition 1. Alexandria VA: Jane's Information Group.

[137] Lydersen, K. (2007, June 21). University accused of lying to hide killing. *The Washington Post.* http://www.washingtonpost.com/wp-dyn/content/article/2007/06/20/AR2007062002172.html

[138] Centers for Disease Control [CDC] (2014 edition). Crisis and Emergency Risk Communication. Available online at: https://www.google.com/url?sa=t&rct=j&q=&esrc=s&source=web&cd=1&cad=rja&uact=8&ved=2ahUKEwjl1-yH3eLiAhVShuAKHVXjBcAQFjAAegQIABAC&url=https%3A%2F%2Femergency.cdc.gov%2Fcerc%2Fresources%2Fpdf%2Fcerc_2014edition.pdf&usg=AOvVaw2SGMgqsJk0QvMSEuAz3mZQ
Also, CDC. Crisis and Emergency Risk Communication... For Leaders By Leaders. Available online at: http://emergency.cdc.gov/erc/leaders.pdf

[139] https://www.washingtonpost.com/world/national-security/is-this-the-end-of-my-life-false-alert-of-missile-attack-sends-hawaii-scrambling/2018/01/13/78c86054-f8a0-11e7-b34a-b85626af34ef_story.html?utm_term=.ad978abd8c3e

[140] http://newsfeed.time.com/2013/01/24/pee-yew-foul-french-smell-prompts-emergency-calls-3/

[141] https://heavy.com/news/2013/01/funky-french-gas-cloud-makes-england-smell-like-rotten-eggs/

[142] https://melissaagnes.com/an-excellent-example-of-twitter-use-in-atlanta-school-shooting/

[143] https://www.slideshare.net/shanxz/asiana-flight-214-crash-in-sfo-crises-management-case-study-and-analysis

[144] http://www.kamenko.com/news/politics/washington-politics/ashcroft-addresses-employees-at-the-justice-department
https://www.cbsnews.com/news/cover-up-at-justice-department/

[145] https://www.bluebell.com/get-the-scoop/#press-releases
https://www.adweek.com/digital/blue-bell-creameries-ceo-issues-video-apology-for-listeria-cases/

[146] https://www.youtube.com/watch?v=n7MfXAaFUIY

[147] https://www.facebook.com/cdllife/posts/957935200896092

[148]
http://www.landlinemag.com/story.aspx?storyid=68093#.XQBeYy2ZOL8

[149] https://www.cbsnews.com/news/police-man-with-assault-rifle-dc-comet-pizza-victim-of-fake-sex-trafficking-story/
https://www.rollingstone.com/politics/politics-news/anatomy-of-a-fake-news-scandal-125877/

[150] http://blog.amtrak.com/2015/05/message-president-ceo-joe-boardman-train-188/

[151] Centers for Disease Control [CDC] (2014 edition). Crisis and Emergency Risk Communication. Available online at:
https://www.google.com/url?sa=t&rct=j&q=&esrc=s&source=web&cd=1&cad=rja&uact=8&ved=2ahUKEwjl1-yH3eLiAhVShuAKHVXjBcAQFjAAegQIABAC&url=https%3A%2F%2Femergency.cdc.gov%2Fcerc%2Fresources%2Fpdf%2Fcerc_2014edition.pdf&usg=AOvVaw2SGMgqsJk0QvMSEuAz3mZQ
Also, CDC. Crisis and Emergency Risk Communication… For Leaders By Leaders. Available online at: http://emergency.cdc.gov/erc/leaders.pdf

[152] Centers for Disease Control [CDC] (2014 edition). Crisis and Emergency Risk Communication. Available online at: https://www.google.com/url?sa=t&rct=j&q=&esrc=s&source=web&cd=1&cad=rja&uact=8&ved=2ahUKEwjl1-yH3eLiAhVShuAKHVXjBcAQFjAAegQIABAC&url=https%3A%2F%2Femergency.cdc.gov%2Fcerc%2Fresources%2Fpdf%2Fcerc_2014edition.pdf&usg=AOvVaw2SGMgqsJk0QvMSEuAz3mZQ
Also, CDC. Crisis and Emergency Risk Communication… For Leaders By Leaders. Available online at: http://emergency.cdc.gov/erc/leaders.pdf

[153] https://www.washingtonpost.com/local/a-halloween-display-or-a-faux-lynching-a-hanging-figure-creates-tensions-in-a-suburban-neighborhood/2017/10/31/62bdf8d2-be67-11e7-97d9-bdab5a0ab381_story.html?utm_term=.019c019e4d19

[154] https://www.arkema-americas.com/en/social-responsibility/community-outreach/paladin-in-florida

[155] https://www.cornucopia.org/2015/09/neighbors-raise-stink-over-strawberry-farms-pesticide/

[156] https://web.archive.org/web/20190308155930/http://www.floridapesticides.com/andrew-horvath-tribune-report-about-strawberry-pesticide-lsquobiasedrsquo.html

[157] http://newsok.com/article/2748666 https://www.actionpa.org/fluoride/chemicals/catoosa.html

Credits

Cover Design and Graphics: Sheila Kwiatek,
Flower Grafix
eBook Design & Processing: Donna Luther,
Metadata Prime

Philip Jan Rothstein, FBCI, is President of Rothstein Associates Inc., a management consultancy he founded in 1984 as a pioneer in the disciplines of Business Continuity and Disaster Recovery. He is also the Executive Publisher of Rothstein Publishing.

Glyn Davies is Chief Marketing Officer of Rothstein Associates Inc. He has held this position since 2013. Glyn has previously held executive level positions in Sales, Marketing and Editorial at several multinational publishing companies and currently resides in California.

Rothstein Publishing is your premier source of books and learning materials about Business Resilience, including Crisis Management, Business Continuity, Disaster Recovery, Emergency Management, Security, Cybersecurity and Risk Management, as well as related fields including Root Cause Analysis and Critical Infrastructure. Our industry-leading authors provide current, actionable knowledge, solutions, and tools you can put in practice immediately. Rothstein Publishing remains true to the decades-long commitment of Rothstein Associates, which is to prepare you and your organization to protect, preserve, and recover what is most important: your people, facilities, assets, and reputation.

info@rothstein.com
www.rothstein.com

ABOUT THE AUTHOR

Dr. Jo Robertson has a doctoral degree in crisis management and more than 20 years of experience keeping companies out of crisis.

As Global Director of Emergency Preparedness for Capital One, she was responsible for orchestrating the creation of a coordinated universal emergency preparedness program with a strong and consistent process as well as the leadership of 2500 life safety team members.

As Director of Crisis Preparedness for Arkema, she rebuilt and re-energized US crisis preparedness initiatives for France's leading chemicals producer. She was responsible for creating an effective corporate crisis management team process and strategy, media training and community relations assistance for the plants as well as acting as a trusted advisor to C-Suite executives.

At Deloitte Services, Dr. Robertson led the national crisis management program for 100+ offices of 45,000+ professionals. She developed Deloitte's enterprise crisis management and crisis communications plans as well as hundreds of local office business continuity plans.

As Vice President for Marsh Crisis Consulting (formerly the Corporate Response Group) she designed, developed and delivered a wide array of services for senior corporate and C-Suite clients, including crisis communications planning, media training, real-time support for clients currently in crisis, and complex crisis management exercises for global and domestic pharmaceutical, petroleum, chemical, energy, banking, hotel, distribution, manufacturing, consumer goods, food service, and government sector clients.

Dr. Robertson spent the first half of her career as a television journalist. She is experienced in all aspects of television news, including producing, writing, and editing. She covered the White House, Pentagon, State Department and Capitol Hill and was responsible for news stories which initiated change at the highest levels of government, including a reversal of policy at the Pentagon.

Dr. Robertson has a doctoral degree in Crisis Management (George Washington University), an M.A. in Journalism (American University), and a B.A. in Communications (Pennsylvania State University).

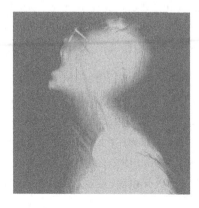

Made in the USA
Las Vegas, NV
29 May 2021